AIR WAR ON THE EASTERN FRONT

CASEMATE | ILLUSTRATED

CASEMATE | ILLUSTRATED

AIR WAR ON THE EASTERN FRONT

MIKE GUARDIA

CASEMATE | ILLUSTRATED

For Marie and Melanie

CIS0019

Print Edition: ISBN 978-1-61200-9087
Digital Edition: ISBN 978-1-61200-9094

Design by Battlefield Design
Color profiles by Ronny Bar
Printed and bound in the Czech Republic by FINIDR, s.r.o.

CASEMATE PUBLISHERS (US)
Telephone (610) 853-9131
Fax (610) 853-9146
Email: casemate@casematepublishers.com
www.casematepublishers.com

CASEMATE PUBLISHERS (UK)
Telephone (01865) 241249
Fax (01865) 794449
Email: casemate-uk@casematepublishers.co.uk
www.casematepublishers.co.uk

Photo credits: Scott Pick WWII Russian Front Original Photo Collection—via Anthony Tucker-Jones, San Diego Air and Space Museum, Russian Ministry of Defense, Russian Air Force, German Federal Archives, Polish National Archives, Hungarian National Archives, United States Air Force, Finnish Wartime Photograph Archive—SA kuva, Russian International News Agency (RIA Novosti), Corwin-Kerber, Ovcharenko Archive, Bedin Denis Yurevich, Suren Migranovich Kafafyan, Medin Robănescu.

Title page: Stukas in flight over the Eastern Front, December 22, 1943.
Contents page: : Il-2s in action over the Kursk salient.
Map: The disposition of the Luftwaffe's expeditionary forces on the eve of Operation *Barbarossa*, the German invasion of the Soviet Union. The combined forces were sufficient to penetrate deep into the Soviet homeland, but as the harsh Russian winter descended upon the Luftwaffe (and the Soviets began rolling back Nazi forces), the Luftwaffe had to divert many of its assets from the North African theater.

Note: aircraft illustrations and profiles are not to scale.

Contents

Timeline of Events

June 1941: Having conquered most of Western Europe, Adolf Hitler turned his attention to the vast Soviet Union. Disregarding his Non-Aggression Pact with Joseph Stalin, Hitler launched Operation *Barbarossa*, a full-scale invasion of the Soviet homeland—aimed squarely at Moscow. In the skies over Russia, the battle-hardened airmen of the Luftwaffe made short work of the Red Air Force during the opening days of *Barbarossa*. To make matters worse, Stalin had executed many of his best pilots during the perennial purges of the 1930s. Thus, much of the Red Air Force was destroyed on the ground before meeting the Luftwaffe in the skies. By 1944, however, the Soviet airmen had regained the initiative and fervently wrested air superiority from the now-ailing Axis Powers.

1941

June 22, 1941: Operation *Barbarossa* opens. The Wehrmacht invades the Soviet Union.

August 1941: Production of the Yakovlev Yak-7 fighter commences.

September 8, 1941: The siege of Leningrad begins.

October 2, 1941: The battle of Moscow begins.

December 1941: During the initial Soviet counteroffensive near Moscow, the Red Air Force gains air superiority over the Luftwaffe for the first time.

1942

January 7, 1942: The battle of Moscow comes to an end with a Soviet victory. End of *Barbarossa*.

August 23, 1942: The battle of Stalingrad begins. 16th Soviet Air Army deploys 10 fighter regiments.

September 1942: Luftflotte 4 conducts more than 1,000 sorties per day against enemy positions in Stalingrad.

October 5, 1942: Ju 87 Stukas from Luftflotte 4 fly nearly 900 sorties against Soviet positions at the Stalingrad Tractor Factory. Several Soviet ground regiments are destroyed.

November 8, 1942: Luftflotte 4 is withdrawn from the Eastern Front to combat the Allied landings in North Africa.

1943

January 31–February 2, 1943: German 6th Army is finally destroyed at Stalingrad. The Luftwaffe loses more than 900 aircraft during the battle.

A flight of Bf 109s in formation over the Eastern Front. By 1943, although still a champion fighter of the Luftwaffe, the Bf 109 was beginning to meet its match against the latter-day variants of the Yakovlev and Lavochkin fighters.

July 5, 1943: The battle of Kursk begins. 32nd GIAP takes delivery of new Lavochkin La-5 fighter in time for the battle.

January 27, 1944: The siege of Leningrad is lifted after nearly three years.

June 22, 1944: Operation *Bagration* opens under Zhukov. Over 1.2 million Soviet troops go into action along four fronts.

January 13, 1945: The East Prussian Offensive opens. Some 3,000 Soviet aircraft partake in one of the final thrusts into Nazi Germany.

April 30, 1945: As the Red Army closes in on Berlin, Hitler commits suicide.

May 7, 1945: Nazi Germany surrenders.

1944

1945

Il-2s from the 16th Air Army prepare to get airborne on another strafing run against German armored units.

Prelude to the Great Patriotic War

In the opening days of the Eastern Front, the Red Air Force seemed to be on the verge of collapse. Indeed, entire airfields were wiped out as the Luftwaffe pummeled Stalin's air forces. On the ground, it appeared that the Red Army wasn't faring much better. Within months of the opening volleys, the Wehrmacht had trampled the Soviets' frontier defenses—occupying some of the most economically and strategically critical areas of the Soviet Union. By the fall of 1941, the Germans had come within sight of Moscow. Despite these early successes, however, the German offensive stalled with the onset of the harsh Russian winter. Hitler had expected a quick and easy victory. What he received, however, was a debilitating war of attrition for which he and his field marshals were grossly unprepared.

A Morane-Saulnier G monoplane. This French-built sport aircraft was among the earliest planes acquired by the Imperial Russian Air Force during World War I.

Following the battle of Moscow, the Soviet counteroffensive began pushing the Wehrmacht back towards the borders of the Fatherland. As Nazi Germany began diverting more of its attention towards the incoming British and American forces, the Wehrmacht could no longer remain a viable force along Eastern Front—either on the ground or in the air. Subsequent operations to regain the initiative against Soviet forces ended in failure, which eventually led to the Wehrmacht's final collapse.

The Eastern Front was a conflict more than 20 years in the making. Both Germany and the Soviet Union had been suffering from internal strife since the end of World War I. The latter-day Russian Empire had withdrawn from the conflict in 1917, as Czar Nicholas II tried to stem the tide of the revolution erupting within his kingdom. Unable to counter the political unrest, he abdicated his throne and was placed under house arrest by the revolutionary government. The Czar and his family, however, were later executed, in July 1918, by Bolshevik revolutionaries. Following a brief civil war in which the "Red" Bolsheviks won, Vladimir Lenin and his communist acolytes proclaimed a new "Union of Soviet Socialist Republics"—commonly referred to as the Soviet Union. By the mid-1920s, Joseph

A prototype of the Polikarpov I-5 fighter (codenamed "VT-11") at a Soviet airfield, April 28, 1930. The Polikarpov I-series planes were among the first and most prominent of the domestically built Soviet aircraft.

Stalin had emerged as the supreme leader of the USSR, and ruled the communist nation with a brand of brutality that far exceeded anything under Czarist rule. Among his many crimes against humanity, Stalin regularly murdered Soviet citizens whom he deemed "disloyal" to his regime. These perennial "purges" targeted private citizens and government officials alike. These dastardly executions diminished the ranks of the Soviet military, foolishly depriving the Red Army and Red Air Force of their best and brightest officers.

The situation in Germany, meanwhile, hadn't been much better. Emerging defeated from World War I, Germany struggled to find its way through the post-war chaos under the fragile leadership of the Weimar Republic. As the economic hardship of the 1920s gave way to political unrest, a failed artist named Adolf Hitler founded the National Socialist German Workers' (Nazi) Party. Channeling his personal charisma and firebrand rhetoric, Hitler successfully played upon Germany's collective attitude of defeat and shame. Promising prosperity, and revenge against the former Allied Powers of yesteryear, Hitler molded Germany into a single-party fascist dictatorship under the Nazi banner. Disregarding the Treaty of Versailles, Hitler rearmed the German military and proceeded to annex Austria and part of Czechoslovakia. Deciding that Germany needed to flex its muscles, Hitler ordered the Wehrmacht to invade Poland on September 1, 1939—thus initiating World War II. Over the ensuing year, Britain and France tried to stem the tide of Nazi aggression as Hitler invaded Belgium, the Netherlands, Denmark, and Norway. France fell to Germany in 1940, and Britain may have fallen as well, if not for the bravery of the Royal Air Force (RAF). In aerial skirmishes big and small, RAF pilots defeated the Luftwaffe in the battle of Britain, thwarting Hitler's plan to conquer the British Isles.

Meanwhile, as Stalin perpetrated his own crimes against the Soviet people, he took note of his fellow dictator on the other side of Europe. Stalin, not one for making friends in the West, saw an opportunity in building an alliance with Nazi Germany. Wanting to maintain Soviet neutrality, Stalin hoped that Germany's war with Britain and France would eventually exhaust all three nations, thus paving the way for Soviet dominance on mainland Europe. What Stalin hadn't anticipated, however, was Germany's abrupt invasion of the Soviet homeland. On June 22, 1941, German forces crossed the border into the Soviet Union. Operation *Barbarossa*—and the war along the Eastern Front—had just begun.

In Russia, Operation *Barbarossa* was the start of what became known as the "Great Patriotic War." The battles along the Eastern Front constituted the largest, continuous military operation in history. Of the nearly 80 million deaths attributed to World War II, nearly 30 million occurred on the Eastern Front. This theater of war produced many of the conflict's largest and most destructive battles. The Eastern Front produced the war's highest casualties and, arguably, the worst atrocities. Of the major combatants during World War II, the Soviet Union suffered the highest number of casualties. Indeed, more than 21 million Soviet citizens lost their lives during the Great Patriotic War—nearly 8 million of whom were non-combatant civilians.

The Red Air Force

The Red Air Force, officially known as the Voyenno-Vozdushnye Sily (VVS; literal translation: "Military Air Forces"), traced its origins to the Imperial Russian Air Service (IRAS) of the World War I era. Established in 1912 at the behest of Czar Nicholas II, the IRAS began as part of the Russian Army with less than a handful of aircraft. Growing steadily throughout its inaugural year, the IRAS saw its first action during the Balkan War of 1912–13, wherein a detachment of four Russian pilots and six technicians served alongside the Bulgarian forces.

At the outset of World War I, the IRAS numbered some 263 aircraft and 14 dirigible airships, making it the second-largest air force behind France. Most of the Russian crates, however, were obsolete by Western standards. Initially, the IRAS used its aircraft for reconnaissance and for coordinating artillery fire. It was not until later that the Russian high command saw fit to modify its planes to attack ground targets or carry bombs. Even the art of dogfighting was slow to take hold within the IRAS. For during the early years of its operation, the IRAS armed its pilots with 7.63mm Mauser C96 pistols. Indeed, many thought it was more practical to shoot an opposing pilot from the open cockpit with a pistol. Some Russian pilots even carried carbines aboard their biplanes.

During the opening volleys against the Central Powers, Russian pilots distinguished themselves on a number of levels. For example, on September 8, 1914, Lieutenant Pyotr Nesterov executed the first aerial ramming attack in history. As Russian planes were still unarmed at this point, the 27-year-old Nesterov rammed his Morane-Saulnier Type G aircraft into an Austro-Hungarian Albatros B.II reconnaissance aircraft flown by Franz Malina and Baron Friedrich von Rosenthal. Shortly thereafter, Lieutenant Vyacheslav Tkachov became the first Russian pilot to shoot down an enemy aircraft with a *handgun*, downing a German Albatros.

In January 1915, the Czar's Ministry of War began arming its planes with 7.62mm Madsen light machine guns and 7.71mm Lewis light machine guns. By this point, it had become clear that onboard machine guns could down an enemy aircraft quicker than a handheld pistol or carbine rifle. Although the other participating air forces were making similar adaptations, it signaled a new era in military aviation—the veritable birth of air-to-air combat.

Over the next two years, the burgeoning IRAS continued to distinguish itself in combat. More than 260 Russian aviators were decorated for valor—26 of whom were designated "aces" of the Russian Empire. The most successful Russian pilot of the war was Alexander Kazakov—credited with shooting down 20 enemy planes.

The success of the IRAS, however, was short-lived. By 1917, Russian forces had, on the whole, performed poorly in the field. Frustration over the apparent military failures, and a growing discontent with the Czar's domestic policies, led to the February Revolution, and Russia's subsequent withdrawal from World War I. The subsequent October Revolution plunged the Russian Empire into the arms of the Bolsheviks and their attendant Marxist-Leninist ideologies.

German officers inspect two captured Soviet aircraft, including a Yakovlev UT-1 trainer (foreground) and a damaged Polikarpov I-16, summer 1941. The I-16 was a resilient Soviet fighter that featured prominently during the inaugural year of the Great Patriotic War.

As the communists consolidated their power, and established the Union of Soviet Socialist Republics, the latter-day IRAS became the "Workers' and Peasants' Red Air Fleet," and finally the "Military Air Forces of the USSR." As the Soviet Union emerged on the international stage, Stalin made wide-sweeping efforts to modernize the aircraft and hone the professionalism of the Red Air Force. Many of these efforts were spearheaded by the charismatic young general, Yakov Alksnis, one of the prominent commanders-in-chief of the early Red Air Force. According to Soviet defector Alexander Barmine, General Alksnis was "a man of method and brought a wholly new spirit into Soviet aviation. It is chiefly owing to him that the Air Force is the powerful weapon it is today." Both a leader and technocrat,

Alksnis was instrumental in establishing one of the first Soviet design bureaus—staffed, ironically, by inmates from Butyrki prison, including Nikolai Polikarpov. In 1931, the new design bureau, now based at Khodynka Field, produced the prototype for the Polikarpov I-5 fighter. In recognition of his talent and merit, Alksnis was appointed Commander of the Red Air Forces that same year, while Nikolai Polikarpov and some of his design staffers were released on amnesty. Under Alksnis's leadership, the Red Air Force grew to possess the world's largest bomber force. Meanwhile, aircraft production soared to 8,000 units by the end of 1936. Tragically, Alksnis became a victim of Stalin's Great Purge, and was executed in 1938 on the flimsy charge of aiding and abetting a "Latvian fascist organization."

While the Soviet population suffered under the reign of Stalinist terror, the Soviet aircraft industry, however, continued to flourish. Indeed, the 1930s would witness the rise of many aircraft bureaus that would become synonymous with Russian aviation—Ilyushin, Mikoyan-Gurevich, Lavochkin, Yakovlev, and Sukhoi. Each "design bureau," as they were called, submitted plans for a variety of military aircraft, all with the purpose of achieving parity with the West.

From its earliest days, the Red Air Force followed nearly the same organizational structure as the Soviet ground forces. By the end of the 1930s, the Red Air Force was descendingly organized into air armies, aviation corps, aviation divisions, and aviation regiments. The regiments were further subdivided into squadrons, flights, and fire teams.

The Lavochkin-Gorbunov-Gudkov LaGG-3 was, in 1941, one of the most modern aircraft available to the Red Air Force. However, the plane was constructed of wood, it was overweight for a fighter, and it was terribly underpowered. Due to these design problems, the LaGG-3 was later superseded by the Lavochkin La-5 and La-7 fighters.

Pilots of the Red Air Force had their first baptism by fire in the skies over Spain. During the Spanish Civil War, the Soviets rendered aid to the left-leaning Republican forces in their struggle against Franco's Nationalists. Meanwhile, Nazi Germany provided military aid to Franco's forces—thus giving the Germans and the Soviets an opportunity to see how each's aircraft would stack up against the other. At first, the Polikarpov I-16 fared better than any fighter in the Luftwaffe, until the arrival of the Messerschmitt Bf 109 fighters. To make matters worse, the Red Air Force had supplied so few I-16s, that its initial air victories were soon squandered as the German-equipped forces gained strength in numbers. Thus, the combination of numerical superiority and the game-changing Bf 109 meant that Franco's Nationalists would soon control the skies over Spain. The defeat of the Soviet-backed Republicans in Spain coincided with the Great Purge of 1938—in which Stalin murdered the best and brightest of his own officer corps. The untimely demise of his most experienced officers severely impacted the combat vitality of the Red Air Force. Young and newly promoted officers attempted to fill these manpower gaps, but these young officers often lacked flying and command experience. Meanwhile, the older commanders who had survived the purge—witnessing the fate of their comrades like Yakov Alksnis—became automatons who dared not take initiative beyond the procedural scripts provided by Moscow.

The first major reorganization of the Red Air Force began in 1939, to bring it more in line with the structure of their ground-based counterparts in the Red Army. For example, in 1939, the "air brigade" was abolished and replaced with the new, aforementioned aviation regiment. An aviation regiment was classified according to its function: bomber, fighter, or ground attack (the latter commonly referred to as "Shturmovik" regiments, which were equipped primarily with the Ilyushin Il-2).

Every bomber regiment contained five squadrons, with 12 aircraft assigned to each squadron. Every fighter regiment contained four squadrons, with 15 aircraft each. The ground-attack regiments shared the same configuration as the fighter regiments. Regardless of its comparative function, however, each regiment contained 60 aircraft in total. Bomber regiments were further categorized according to their type: fast bomber, dive bomber, light bomber, close-support bomber, long-range bomber, or heavy bomber.

At the next highest echelon, the air division contained between four to six air regiments. Air divisions themselves could be "pure" or "composite." A pure air division operated one exclusive type of aircraft—fighter, bomber, or ground-attack. Composite air divisions, on the other hand, contained of a mix of fighter and bomber regiments and were often attached directly to a corresponding ground army.

The Soviet military was also unique in that its Air Force and Air Defense Forces were two distinct branches, each on par with the Army and Navy. The Air Defense Forces were officially known as the "Protivovozdushnaya Oborona Strany," (literally "Anti-Air Defense of the Nation"), or PVO for short. As their name implied, the PVO was responsible for anti-aircraft artillery in defense of the Soviet homeland. However, the PVO also had a number of fighter regiments assigned to its various corps-level units. These regiments often flew planes like the Mikoyan-Gurevich MiG-3 and Yakovlev Yak-1.

Despite this formidable structure, the Red Air Force (and its brethren in the PVO) was still woefully understrength by the summer of 1941. Before the start of Operation *Barbarossa*,

Luftwaffe intelligence concluded that the average Soviet fighter and ground-attack regiment had only 48 aircraft against an authorized strength of 60. These same analysts determined that the bomber and reconnaissance regiments were in even worse condition—averaging nearly 36 aircraft among each formation. Come what may, these numbers did not reflect an optimistic assessment for Stalin's air force.

Soviet Aircraft

Ilyushin Il-2 Shturmovik

Among the most prominent Soviet planes of World War II was Ilyushin's Il-2. Like most aircraft in the Soviet military, the plane's nominal prefix took the first two letters of its manufacturer, "Il," followed by a serial number designating its relative position in the sequence of planes produced by that bureau. Iluyshin was one of several Soviet aircraft manufacturers established during the 1930s. Founded in 1933 by aerospace engineer Sergey Ilyushin, the Ilyushin Design Bureau assumed the task of creating a highly maneuverable attack aircraft for the ever-expanding Red Air Force.

The Ilyushin Il-2 was perhaps the most famous Soviet aircraft of World War II. Known as the "Shturmovik," the Il-2 was a fierce ground-attack aircraft—aptly nicknamed the "Flying Tank."

With more than 36,000 units produced during the war, Il-2 is the single-most-produced military aircraft in aviation history. To its pilots, the aircraft was simply known as the "Ilyusha." To the soldiers on the ground, however, it was the "Flying Tank"—a near-indestructible plane that could deliver a fearsomely heavy punch from the third dimension. Its official nickname, however, was the "Shturmovik" (literal translation: "attack plane"). Throughout the war, it provided such critical support to Soviet ground troops that Stalin himself remarked that the Il-2 was "as essential to the Red Army as air and bread."

Prior to its inaugural flight on October 2, 1939, however, the Il-2 had been confronted by fierce competition from the other Soviet design bureaus. For example, Dmitry Grigorovich (who had worked alongside Polikarpov for the development of the I-5 fighter) designed the TSh-1 and TSh-2 armored attack planes. At the time of their unveiling, however, Soviet aircraft engines did not have the power necessary to make heavier planes like the TSh reliable in combat. Attempting to reconcile the need for armored protection against the need for high-performance aerodynamics, Sergey Ilyushin and his design team created the first Il-2 prototype, codenamed the "TsKB-55." It was a two-seater aircraft with a 1,540-pound armored shell encasing the fuselage—protecting both the crew and the vital components of the plane. Fully loaded, the Il-2 weighed more than 10,000 pounds, with the armored shell accounting for nearly 15 percent of the aircraft's gross weight. The monocoque construction was unique in that the armored casing was designed as a load-bearing part of the plane's structure, thus saving considerable weight to the overall airframe. Ultimately, the Red Air Force selected Ilyushin's design over the Sukhoi Su-6, giving the former a new designation of "BSh-2" ("Bronirovani Shturmovik," translated: armored ground attack).

This BSh-2 prototype, however, was overweight and underpowered. Undaunted, Ilyushin redesigned the prototype with a single-seat design and a Mikulin AM-38 powertrain delivering more than 1,600 horsepower. This new prototype, branded the "TsKB-57" took its maiden flight on October 12, 1940. The production-series aircraft then passed State Acceptance Trials in March 1941, and was officially redesignated the "Il-2" the following month. The Ilyushin Il-2 was subsequently delivered to operational units in May 1941.

The armament was perhaps the most impressive feature of the Il-2. Indeed, the Shturmovik featured the Volkov-Yartsev VYa-23, a deadly 23mm autocannon, a common accoutrement found on the World War II-era Soviet planes. Developed in 1940, the VYa-23 was intended to penetrate enemy armor. A gas-operated, belt-fed behemoth, the autocannon fired 600 rounds per minute—an impressively high rate of fire for a weapon of that caliber. Although fast and powerful, the gun was not without its drawbacks. For example, the strong recoil and the quick-draw function of the chambering mechanism often led to jams and misfires that could not be fixed during flight.

Despite these drawbacks, the Il-2 performed admirably in combat and was well liked by the crews who flew it. Although the "TsKB-57" variant had a single-seat cockpit, all future iterations of the Il-2 were two-seaters. The Il-2 entered series production at four aircraft factories in early 1941—including State Aviation Factory 18 in Voronezh and Factory 381 in Leningrad. After the war, the Il-2 remained in service with the Soviet Union and other Eastern Bloc air forces until well into the 1950s.

In Profile:
Il-2 and La-5

The Ilyushin Il-2 "Shturmovik" was perhaps the most renowned Soviet aircraft of the war. A fierce ground-attack aircraft, the Il-2 was known for its rugged survivability, often nicknamed the "Flying Tank."

The Lavochkin La-5. Though not quite on par with the Bf 109 or Fw 190, the La-5 was still a respectable fighter. The successive "La-5F" and "La-5FN" variants were a marked improvement over the original airframe. A further iteration, the La-7, was renowned as one of the toughest fighters on the Eastern Front.

Lavochkin La-5 and La-7

Of the prominent Soviet and Russian aerospace firms, Lavochkin is often overshadowed by its "big brothers:" Tupelov, Mikoyan-Gurevich, and Sukhoi. Indeed, World War II was the highwater mark for Lavochkin's reign as an aerospace giant. By the dawn of the Cold War, Lavochkin was among the first design bureaus to develop fighter jets for the Red Air Force. However, none of their designs could compete against the forthcoming generation of MiGs and Sukhois. By the 1960s, Lavochkin had shifted its focus to developing missiles and spacecraft. During the Great Patriotic War, however, Lavochkin delivered what was perhaps the most prominent fighters of the Red Air Force: the La-5 and its derivative La-7.

The Lavochkin La-5 was a great step forward in Soviet fighter aircraft. Arriving on the Eastern Front in mid-1942, the La-5 was the first Soviet plane that could truly hold its own against the Focke-Wulfe Fw 190 and Messerschmitt Bf 109.

The La-5 itself was an iteration of the earlier LaGG-3, a wooden monoplane whose size, weight, and underpowered engine made it a liability in the skies over Russia. Shortly after its introduction in 1941, the LaGG-3's shortcomings caused Lavochkin to fall out of favor with Stalin and the Soviet high command. Factories that had previously been designated to build the LaGG-3 were turned over to the rival design bureau Yakovlev, to build the Yak-1 and Yak-7. Undaunted, Lavochkin unofficially began refining the LaGG-3 into the new prototype La-5.

When the La-5 prototype took its maiden flight in March 1942, evaluators were pleasantly surprised. The performance and handling of the La-5 stood head and shoulders above the LaGG-3. The improved powertrain had enabled Lavochkin's crate to achieve the performance metrics necessary for a contemporary fighter. In fact, the Soviet test pilots were so impressed by the La-5, that they declared it superior to the Yak-7.

By July 1942, the La-5 was in mass production at factories in Moscow and Yaroslav. Although still inferior to the Germans' Bf-109 at higher altitudes, the La-5 was a fearsome opponent in dogfights closer to the ground. Because most of the aerial battles over the Eastern Front took place at altitudes below 16,000 feet, the La-5 was decisively in its element.

Further modifications to the aircraft included cutting down the rear fuselage to give the pilot better visibility. This modified version was designated the La-5F. A later version, the La-5FN, featured a fuel-injected engine and a lighter gross weight. The La-5FN would become the definitive version of the aircraft.

The earliest versions of the La-5 carried two 20mm ShVAK gas-operated autocannons, capable of firing 700–800 rounds per minute. Late production-model La-5FNs, on the other hand, featured two 20mm Berezin B-20 autocannons, which conserved weight without sacrificing muzzle velocity or a high rate of fire. Although reliable and well liked by its pilots, the La-5 was not without its drawbacks. Neither the engine nor the cockpit was well ventilated. Due to poor insulation, exhaust fumes from the engine often seeped into the cockpit. Consequently, La-5 pilots often flew with their canopies open.

Nevertheless, Lavochkin's fighter earned a solid reputation among Soviet pilots. Said former fighter pilot Viktor Sinaisky:

> That was an excellent fighter with two cannons and a powerful air-cooled engine. The first La-5s from the Tbilisi factory were slightly inferior, while the last ones from the Gorki plant, which came to us from Ivanovo, were perfect. At first, we received regular La-5s, but then we got new ones containing the ASh-82FN engine with direct injection of fuel into the cylinders. It was perfected and had better maneuverability, acceleration, speed, and climb rate compared to the early variants. Everyone was in love with the La-5. It was easy to maintain, too.

Nearly 10,000 La-5s were built by the end of the war. The La-5 remained in service among several Eastern Bloc air forces following World War II. Today, a number of La-5 replicas are on display. However, the last surviving *original* La-5 remains in storage at the Military Aviation Museum in Virginia Beach, Virginia.

The Lavochkin La-7 was built upon the improvements made to the latter-day La-5. Although the La-5 had become a mainstay of the Red Air Force's fighter squadrons, its chief designer, Semyon Lavochkin, felt that the plane could be improved. Among its many refinements, Lavochkin sealed the engine cowling, rearranged the wing center section to accommodate a new oil cooler, and made further adjustments to improve the pilot's visibility. With these modifications to the La-5, Lavochkin dubbed it the "La-7."

Debuting in 1944, the La-7 improved upon the earlier La-5. Many pilots considered the La-7 to be on par with the best of the Luftwaffe's fighter aircraft. The La-7 remained in service with the Red Air Force until 1947.

Initial flight tests during the winter of 1943/4 showed exceptional performance. While using the same engine as the earlier La-5FN, the new La-7 prototype reached top speeds in excess of 420 miles per hour. This was 40 miles per hour faster than the newest production-model La-5FN. The new La-7 could also climb faster and attain better airspeeds at higher altitudes. Whereas the La-5's body had been made from wood (mostly to conserve strategic metals for other wartime products), Lavochkin was able to incorporate more alloy-based components into the La-7. Indeed, by 1944, Soviet strategists had determined that there was a sufficient supply of metal to ease the restrictions on its use. Incorporating these alloys understandably made the La-7 more resilient in the air.

Factory 381 in Moscow, which had been manufacturing the La-5FN, fully transitioned into producing the new La-7 by May 1944. More than 5,000 La-7s were built by the time production ended in 1946. After the war, the La-7 remained in Soviet service until it was phased out by the end of the decade. The La-7's only foreign operator was the Czechoslovakian Air Force, which held the plane in service until 1950.

Yakovlev Yak 1/3/7/9

Yakovlev's Yak-series fighters were among the most prolific Soviet aircraft of World War II. The Yak-1, Yak-3, Yak-7, and Yak-9 were all produced within a few years of one another, and several of their production runs overlapped. Each of the four fighters had the same basic design, with various upgrades and modifications to the successively numbered variants. The Yakovlev Design Bureau was the namesake of its founder, Alexander Yakovlev, a prominent aerospace engineer and eventual Vice-Minister of Aviation under Joseph Stalin. Still in

Commander of the 16th Air Army, Lieutenant General S.I. Rudenko, stands in front of a Yakovlev Yak-1 fighter, 1943. The early Yak-series fighters featured prominently along the Eastern Front. However, the Yakovlev fighters could not truly stand toe to toe against the Luftwaffe until the development of the Yak-7 and Yak-9.

existence as a division of the modern-day Irkut Corporation, Yakovlev has produced some of the most notable military and civil aircraft of the former Eastern Bloc.

Produced in 1940, the Yak-1 was a single-seat monoplane known for its speed and maneuverability. Prior to the war, the Yakovlev Design Bureau was best known for its lightweight sport aircraft. However, Yakovlev's tactical bomber had so impressed the Red Air Force that Stalin ordered the bureau to design a new fighter. Although the initial design seemed promising, and capitalized on Yakovlev's prior experience with manufacturing agile sports aircraft, the Yak-1 prototypes, however, were plagued by mechanical problems—including overheated motor oil and issues with the landing gear. These and other technical issues led to the Yak-1 prototype's failure during the opening rounds of government testing in 1940. Fortunately for Yakovlev, its competitors, Mikoyan-Gurevich and Lavochkin, had also failed their initial testing. Mikoyan-Gurevich had tested the "I-200" (which later became the MiG-3), while Lavochkin had submitted its "I-301" (the future LaGG-3). As Yakovlev returned to the "drawing board," designers incorporated several improvements, producing an updated prototype which was delivered for testing in October 1940. Although the Yak-1 passed government testing in December 1940, the plane was still in need of refinement, and its engine remained problematic.

The delivery of the Yak-1 was somewhat complicated because the plane entered mass production while it was still being tested and refined. Indeed, the Yak-1 went through so many design changes that the assembly lines could barely put together a coherent plane. There were nearly 8,000 modifications made to the Yak-1 blueprints by 1941. Nearly 7,000 additional modifications followed in 1942. Often, this left factory workers with the

A Yakovlev Yak-3 in flight. Noted for its ease of maintenance and high thrust-to-weight ratio, the Yak-3 was a solid performer in the skies over Eastern Europe. From its debut in 1944 until its production end in 1946, more than 4,800 units were built.

unenviable task of trying to cobble together airframes with various parts from different iterations of the Yak-1. Thus, nearly every Yak-1 was unique and the parts were rendered non-interchangeable. The incongruent parts for the ever-evolving Yak-1 prompted several production teams to modify the parts on hand. For example, the left and right landing gear for a particular Yak-1 may have been incongruent as both had been designed for different iterations of the plane. A factory would thus modify one side of the landing gear to ensure an even stance for the aircraft. Despite these manufacturing issues, more than 8,000 Yak-1s were completed by the time production ended in July 1944.

Almost in parallel to the Yak-1, bureau designers began pushing development of the Yak-3. As the Yak-1 prototype was being delivered to Soviet evaluators, Yakovlev simultaneously offered the Yak-3 as an alternate design. The prototype Yak-3 (designated: "I-30") was powered by a Klimov M-105P engine and featured an all-metal airframe, revolutionary for Soviet planes at the time. Like its Yak-1 stablemate, the Yak-3 had a 20mm ShVAK autocannon that fired through a hollow-driveshaft nose spinner. Secondary armaments included two cowl-mounted 7.62mm ShKAS machine guns situated forward of the cockpit on the fuselage. Although Stalin had wanted to push the Yak-3 into production, the scarcity of requisite metals—and the urgency of the Nazi invasion—halted the Yak-3's development in the fall of 1941.

In 1943, however, the Yak-3 unexpectedly found a new lease on life. By this point, the Yak-7 and Yak-9 were already under way, but the Yakovlev Design Bureau made yet another change to its ever-fluid Yak-1. The latest design was dubbed the "Yak-1M" which incorporated a number of aerodynamic refinements, as well as improvements to the engine and armament. In fact, Petr Stefanovskiy, the chief test pilot for the Yak-1M, was so impressed by the new aircraft that he recommended it replace both the Yak-1 *and* Yak-7, while keeping the Yak-9 in production. Instead, the Soviet government redesignated the Yak-1M as the new "Yak-3." The newly fangled Yak-3 entered service in 1944, later than the Yak-9 despite having a lower sequence number. Nearly 5,000 Yak-3s were built before the plane was retired from Soviet service in 1952.

Like the Yak-3, the Yak-7 was also developed from the Yak-1. Initially built as a Yak-1 trainer variant, the Yak-7 was converted to a fighter when it was discovered that its performance metrics were higher than the single-seater Yak-1. Armament testing further concluded that the Yak-7 was a superior firing platform to even the MiG-3. Entering production in the fall of 1941, the first batch of 60 Yak-7s arrived on the frontlines that winter. The most produced variant of the Yak-7 was the Yak-7B, with nearly 5,000 units in service by the end of the war. The Yak-7B was well liked by its pilots, most of whom reported that it was easy to fly at any altitude, stable in its handling, and could keep pace with the Bf 109, although it could not climb as fast. Like any Soviet fighter, however, the plane was not without its drawbacks. The external radiators, for example, created considerable drag; the canopy glass was poorly constructed; and the plane needed greater take-off and landing distances than other planes of comparable size.

The Yak-9, meanwhile, drew upon the success of the Yak-7B. Fundamentally an upgraded version of the Yak-7B, the Yak-9 first arrived on the Stalingrad Front in December 1942, where it played a major role in wresting air superiority from the Luftwaffe—particularly the Focke-Wulf Fw 190 and Messerschmitt Bf 109 fighters.

The Yak-9 differed little from its Yak-7B forebearer. The 9-variant, however, featured a smaller rear decking and an improved canopy that enabled the pilot to have all-around visibility. The overall design also permitted higher fuel and payload capacities. These modifications, combined with the all-metal construction, made the Yak-9 fast and highly maneuverable at low and medium altitudes. At more than 16,000 units built, the Yak-9 was one of the most mass-produced fighters of World War II. Formidable in the air, the Yak-9 variants were equipped with either 37mm or 45mm autocannons. The Yak-9B fighter-bomber variant had a modified rack to accommodate 400kg bombs. The long-range escort variants, Yak-9D and Yak-9DD, had additional wing-mounted fuel tanks. These D-variants escorted Allied bombers over Eastern Europe as Soviet ground troops poured into the Fatherland. The Yak-9 remained in production until 1948, and remained in service with the North Korean Air Force into the 1950s.

A Yakovlev Yak-9DD fighter assigned to a special-purpose aviation group operating near Foggia, Italy. The Yak-9 (and its lettered variants) was considered one of the most advanced Soviet fighters of the World War II era.

Before Mikoyan-Gurevich became the standard bearer for all Soviet fighter aircraft, their MiG-3 interceptor had a less-than-admirable record during the Great Patriotic War. Although the MiG-3 performed well at higher altitudes, most air battles along the Eastern Front were low-altitude engagements—wherein the MiG-3 often fell prey to the Bf 109.

Mikoyan-Gurevich MiG-3

Before the MiG-series aircraft became the standard bearer for Soviet and Russian fighters, the designers at Mikoyan-Gurevich struggled to make a viable airplane for the Red Air Force. The abortive MiG-1 had been plagued by numerous design and performance problems. At barely 100 units produced, the problematic MiG was delivered to frontline units in the summer of 1941 before the design issues had been resolved. Most of these MiG-1s were destroyed during the opening days of Operation *Barbarossa*.

The new MiG-3, however, was created to address the shortcomings of the MiG-1. Upgrades to the MiG-3 included a larger fuel tank, a repositioned engine to provide better longitudinal stability, stronger armor to protect the pilot, improved landing gear, and a higher payload capacity.

During the first round of test flight evaluations, the MiG-3 underperformed. Undaunted, Mikoyan-Gurevich made adjustments to the engine and instrumentation and arranged two more test flights between Moscow and Leningrad. This time, the MiG-3 demonstrated its ability to fly distances beyond 1,100 kilometers, flying at 90-percent maximum airspeed and at altitudes in excess of 20,000 feet.

Although a marked improvement over the MiG-1, the MiG-3 pilots still found the plane's performance unacceptable at high altitudes, despite being designed as a high-altitude interceptor. In fact, the very idea of a high-altitude interceptor seemed unnecessary considering most engagements on the Eastern Front occurred at lower altitudes. In lower-altitude dogfights, the MiG-3 often proved inferior against the German Bf 109, and failed to match the performance of its Red Air Force contemporaries. MiG-3 losses throughout the war were the highest in terms of percentages—with more than 1,400 planes lost. These numbers represented nearly 42 percent of all MiG-3s manufactured. The last MiG-3s were withdrawn before the end of the war.

In Profile:
MiG-3 and P-39

The Mikoyan-Gurevich MiG-3. Years before Mikoyan-Gurevich became the standard bearer for Soviet fighter aircraft, the early MiG-series interceptors performed poorly when compared to their Yakovlev, Ilyushin, and Lavochkin stablemates. Although the MiG-3 performed well at higher altitudes, its utility was limited since most aerial engagements occurred at altitudes below 20,000 feet. This MiG-3 belongs to the 177th Fighter Aviation Regiment, Soviet Air Defense Forces.

This P-39 Airacobra was among the many planes donated to the Soviet Union under the Lend-Lease Program. Despite the political and cultural differences between East and West, the Soviet regime happily accepted military donations from Britain and the US. Although the P-39 was derided by American pilots, it was adored by the Soviet aviators who flew it. Ironically, the low-speed, low-altitude nature of air combat along the Eastern Front played to the P-39's strengths—including its hardy construction and menacing firepower. One of the P-39's biggest champions was Aleksandr Pokryshkin, a Soviet ace who scored 20 air-to-air victories in his P-39.

The Petlyakov Pe-2 dive-bomber. Pictured here is the night-fighter variant. Like many of the Red Air Force's planes, the Pe-2 was adapted to a variety of combat roles during the Great Patriotic War.

Petlyakov Pe-2

The Petlyakov Pe-2 was perhaps the most prominent Soviet bomber of the war. Fast, maneuverable, and highly resilient, the Pe-2 performed a variety of missions beyond its designated role as a bomber—it proved successful as a reconnaissance aircraft, night fighter, and even a heavy fighter. At 11,430 units built, it was among the most mass-produced twin-engine bombers of the war. Unlike many of the Soviet Union's World War II-era planes, the Pe-2 remained in widespread service after the war—flying with several Warsaw Pact air forces, whereupon it became known by the NATO Reporting Name "Buck."

Designed by Vladimir Petlyakov in 1937, the Pe-2 was developed as a high-altitude escort fighter. When its first prototype flew in December 1939, it carried many features that were revolutionary for its time, including a pressurized cabin and an all-metal construction. However, shortly before production began, the Red Air Force demanded a redesign of the entire plane. Taking note of the Luftwaffe's tactical bombing operations in the ongoing blitzkrieg, the Red Air Force decided it needed a dive-bomber instead of an escort fighter. Petlyakov's team was given a mere 45 days to complete their redesign. Removing the cabin pressurization, Petlyakov's team added dive brakes and a bombardier's position among other features. The redesigned aircraft first flew on December 15, 1940, and was put into production shortly thereafter.

Despite its ubiquity and versatility, however, the Pe-2's primary armament was inadequate for its mission sets. The onboard 7.62mm ShKAS machine gun had a high rate of fire; however, its caliber was insufficient to penetrate the ever-evolving armor of the Luftwaffe's modern fighters. Meanwhile, the ventral-mounted Berezin UB machine gun had a narrow field of view, restricting the gunner's situational awareness. Another ShKAS was later added to the airframe, and it could be moved between sockets on both sides of the fuselage. Another dorsal Berezin UBT machine gun was added, which purportedly increased the Pe-2's average mission life expectancy by 170 percent.

Tupelov Tu-2

The Tupelov Tu-2 was among the most effective medium bombers of World War II. A twin-engine, daylight bomber, the Tu-2 was a versatile aircraft, adapted to roles including interceptor, torpedo-bomber, and aerial reconnaissance. It was unique among Soviet aircraft in that it could carry a large internal bombload, yet maintain airspeeds comparable to a single-seater fighter. On the Eastern Front, the Tu-2 spearheaded the final offensives into German territory.

Although a veritable bomber, the Tu-2 had a tumultuous development. For example, its designer, Andrei Tupelov, had been imprisoned in 1937 on false charges of espionage against the Soviet Union. Many of his aerospace colleagues sat alongside him in prison, and several more were executed. Not coincidentally, he was released from prison in July 1941, as his aeronautical designs were considered "conduct important to defense work."

While attempting to defend his reputation, Tupelov began work on the Tu-2, powered by twin Shvetsov ASh-82 engines. The powerplants were 14-cylinder, air-cooled radial piston engines, each capable of producing 1,850 horsepower. This gave the Tu-2 a maximum airspeed of 328 miles per hour and a range of more than 1,000 nautical miles. Aside from its internal and external payloads, the Tu-2 carried two 20mm ShVAK autocannons mounted in the wings. These were accompanied by three rear-firing 7.62mm ShKAS machine guns, which in turn were later replaced by three 12.7mm UB machine guns. More than 2,200 variants of the Tu-2 were built by the time production ended in 1948. The bomber remained in Soviet service until 1950, although it continued to serve in the Chinese People's Liberation Army Air Force (PLAAF) through the 1970s.

The Tupelov SB bomber. At more than 6,900 units built by 1941, the SB became one of the Soviets' premier night bombers.

In Profile:
Hermann Göring
January 12, 1893–October 15, 1946

The man who became synonymous with the Luftwaffe began his career as a fighter pilot during World War I. Göring achieved "ace" status during World War I, claiming 22 air-to-air victories and was awarded the coveted Iron Cross. Göring was the commander-in-chief of the Luftwaffe, as well as Hitler's "heir apparent"—ready to take control of Nazi Germany if and when the Führer relinquished his power. In April 1945, with the Third Reich collapsing around him, Göring sent a telegram to Hitler, requesting to assume command of Nazi Germany. Hitler saw the request as an act of treason, and stripped Göring of his leadership in the Luftwaffe. Göring surrendered to Allied forces on May 6, 1945 and was later tried at Nuremberg for his role in Germany's war crimes. He was sentenced to death by hanging, but committed suicide in prison by way of a cyanide capsule on October 15, 1946.

(JG)—typically equipped with the Messerschmitt Bf 109 or Focke-Wulf Fw 190. Dive-bomber units were referred to as *Sturzkampfgeschwader* (StG; *Stuka Geschwader*)—featuring the renowned Junkers Ju 87.

Beneath the Geschwader, the *Gruppe* (plural: *Gruppen*) was the basic autonomous unit of the Luftwaffe. It had no direct equivalent in the Allied air forces, as it was smaller than a wing-sized unit, but larger than a squadron. Gruppen within a Geschwader were designated by Roman numerals—I, II, III, etc—followed by the abbreviated Geschwader designation. For example, the second Gruppe of Sturzkampfgeschwader 3 would be designated II./StG 3.

Each Gruppe contained three *Staffeln* (singular: *Staffel*), similar in functionality to an Allied squadron. Each Staffel had nine to 12 aircraft depending on its function. A Staffel was further divided into three *Schwärme* (singular: *Schwarm*), consisting of four to six aircraft. Schwärme were subdivided differently according to their function. A standard, six-plane bomber Schwarm, for example, was divided into a *Kette* ("chain") of three aircraft each. A fighter Schwarm, on the other hand, typically had four aircraft, and was subdivided into two *Rotten* (singular: *Rotte*) of two aircraft each. The term Rotte was also used to describe a two-plane formation, what Allied air forces typically called a "section"—consisting of a leader and a wingman.

Although the Luftwaffe rapidly overtook Western Europe during the blitzkrieg of 1940, it suffered an enormous setback during the battle of Britain. In the skies over the English Channel, the pride of Hitler's air fleet succumbed to the fury of the Royal Air Force. Abandoning his designs to conquer the British Isles, Hitler turned his attention to the Soviet Union. Although the early stages of the Soviet invasion replicated the rapid success of blitzkrieg, the Luftwaffe began to break under the strain of a two-front war and the relentless fervor of diehard Soviet airmen.

German Aircraft

Junkers Ju 87 "Stuka"

During the early days of blitzkrieg, few aircraft could inspire more terror than the Junkers Ju 87. Nicknamed the "Stuka"—an abbreviation for *Sturzkampfflugzeug* (German for dive-bomber), the Ju 87 came to symbolize Nazi airpower during the opening days of World War II. With its inverted gull wings and fixed-landing gear, the Stuka was one of the most recognizable aircraft of the European Theater. Its most potent weapon, however, was psychological. Its dive-activated air siren, known as the "Jericho Trumpet," produced a dreadful wail that could incite panic in even the most disciplined ground units.

Introduced in 1935, the Stuka made its combat debut in 1936 as a member of the Condor Legion—the Luftwaffe's expeditionary unit during the Spanish Civil War. Three years later, at the outset of World War II, the Stuka spearheaded the invasion into Poland, Norway, and the Low Countries. Around this time, the Stuka was also exported to other Axis air forces—including Italy, Romania, and Bulgaria. The Stuka also fought during the battle of Britain, but these aerial skirmishes over the English Channel revealed several design and performance problems. Its poor maneuverability, low airspeed, and lack of defensive armament made it easy prey for Allied fighters.

Following the battle of Britain, the Stuka required fighter escorts to operate effectively. Despite suffering setbacks during the battle of Britain, the Stuka nevertheless achieved success during the early days of the Eastern Front. During Operation *Barbarossa*, Ju 87s took a heavy toll on Soviet ground troops, breaking up Soviet counterattacks, reducing fortifications, and disrupting Soviet supply lines. Over the next several months, the Stuka dropped several thousand pounds of ordnance on Soviet positions—from the Russian borderlands to Moscow. However, as the Soviets began to roll back the tide of Nazi aggression, the Ju 87 fell victim to the same problems that had plagued it during the battle of Britain. As the Stuka began falling prey to Soviet fighters, it was replaced by the more resilient Focke-Wulf Fw 190.

Throughout its service life, the Stuka underwent several upgrades and successive iterations. Perhaps the most curious Stuka variant to serve on the Eastern Front was the Ju 87G. The G-variant was the final operational version of the Stuka, turning the Ju-87 into a "tank buster." As the tide turned against the Wehrmacht on the Eastern Front, the Luftwaffe adapted the Ju 87 to counter the growing threat from Soviet armored forces. The G-variant was therefore equipped with two 37mm Bordkanone BK autocannons, mounted underneath the wings, each loaded with two six-round magazines of armor-piercing ammunition. With these adaptations, the tank-killing Stuka was nicknamed the *Kanonenvogel* (German for "cannon-bird"), and was enormously successful when piloted by aces like Ernst Rudel. Many of the G-variants were adapted from existing Ju 87Ds. Other Ju 87Ds were modified to include the twin 37mm guns without being fully upgraded to G-variant status.

After the war, the Ju 87 (along with the other Nazi aircraft) was retired, and many were destroyed amidst the "de-Nazification" process. Today, less than a handful of Stukas survive and none are known to be flyable.

Sporting its now-winterized camouflage scheme, this battered Ju 87 receives some much-needed field repairs before being sent back into the fight.

In Profile:
Ju 87G and Bf 109G-2

The Junkers Ju 87G "Stuka." The G-variant of the Stuka was retrofitted with 37mm anti-tank cannons, turning the Luftwaffe's primary dive-bomber into a "tank buster."

Bf 109G-2. The G ("Gustav") variant was the most mass-produced version of the Bf 109, and among the most prominently featured variants fighting on the Eastern Front.

The Messerschmitt Bf 109 was the veritable "jewel in the crown" of the Luftwaffe's fighter forces. A formidable opponent in the sky, the Bf 109 was respected by Axis forces and Allies alike.

Messerschmitt Bf 109

The "jewel in the crown" of the Luftwaffe's fighter force was the Messerschmitt Bf 109. Designed by Willy Messerschmitt and Robert Lusser of Bayerische Flugzeugwerke company during the 1930s, the Bf 109 was the first modern, multirole aircraft of the Luftwaffe. Throughout its service life, the Bf 109 fulfilled the role of interceptor, air superiority fighter, bomber escort, fighter-bomber, ground-attack aircraft, and reconnaissance aircraft. Its designation "Bf" was an acronym for its manufacturer. However, the plane was commonly referred to as the "Me 109" by Allied aircrews even though it never officially carried that designation. At nearly 34,000 units produced, the Bf 109 is the most prolific fighter aircraft in history.

Like many of its contemporaries, the Bf 109 first saw operational service with the expeditionary Condor Legion during the Spanish Civil War. It was also one of the most advanced fighters of its day—featuring an all-metal monocoque airframe, retractable landing gear, and a closed canopy. Powered by a liquid-cooled V12 engine, it was also among the fastest planes of its day. By the end of the war, the Bf 109 was being supplemented by the equally formidable Focke-Wulf Fw 190.

Even as the Luftwaffe began losing airspace to the Red Air Force, the Bf 109 continued racking up aerial victories. After the fall of Nazi Germany, the Bf 109 continued in service with the Spanish Air Force until 1965. Ironically, the Israeli Air Force also maintained a variant of the Bf 109—the Czechoslovakian copy dubbed the "Avia S-199."

A Focke-Wulf Fw 190 (D-9 variant) after being captured by US troops, 1945. The Fw 190, alongside the Bf 109, was the flagship fighter for the Luftwaffe. Many of the Luftwaffe's most successful pilots claimed their kills in the Fw 190.

Focke-Wulf Fw 190

Like its Bf 109 counterpart, the Fw 190 was a single-seat, single-engine fighter aircraft renowned for its speed, resilience, and versatility. Along with the Bf 109, the Fw 190 became the backbone of the Luftwaffe's fighter squadrons. Most operational variants of the Fw 190 were powered by twin-mounted BMW 801 radial engines. This powerplant enabled the Fw 190 to carry larger payloads than the Bf 109. The Fw 190 was well liked by its pilots. In fact, some of the most successful German fighter aces claimed their kills aboard the Fw 190—including Erich Rudorffer, Otto Kittel, and Walter Nowotny.

Early variants of the Fw 190 were an overmatch for Allied fighters but, as the war dragged on, newer versions of the Spitfire and P-51 Mustang bested the Focke-Wulf in aerial combat. Still, throughout its history, the Focke-Wulf delivered great firepower and, according to several pilots, it outperformed the Bf 109 at low and medium altitudes.

An Fw 190 from Jagdgeschwader 4. The Fw 190 had superior firepower compared to its stablemate, the Bf 109. According to several pilots, the Fw 190 also had greater handling and agility. In the skies over Eastern Europe, the Red Air Force's Lavochkin-built fighters seemed to fare the best against the Fw 190 in air-to-air combat.

The Fw 190 arrived on the Eastern Front in the winter of 1942, finding success as both a fighter and, from October 1943 onwards, a ground-attack aircraft, replacing the beleaguered Ju 87 in the latter role. The penultimate versions of the Focke-Wulf arrived in the fall of 1944. Although these latter-day variants achieved true parity with the stable of Allied fighters, they arrived too late to have an impact on the outcome of the war. Like the Bf 109, the vaunted Fw 190 remained in service with a number of foreign air forces after World War II—notably, the Turkish Air Force, which operated the plane until 1949.

Heinkel He 111

Heinkel's He 111 was perhaps the most recognized German bomber of World War II. Designed by Siegfried and Walter Günter at Heinkel Flugzeugwerke in 1934, the He 111 was a medium multirole bomber, noted for its distinctive glass-domed nose. The He 111 was the premier bomber of the Luftwaffe during the early stages of the war, flying alongside the Stuka during the blitzkrieg and doubling as a strategic bomber during the battle of Britain. Its weak defensive armament, however, necessitated the presence of fighter escorts—typically Bf 109s. Nevertheless, the He 111 was a surprisingly resilient aircraft, capable of staying aloft while sustaining heavy damage.

Along the Eastern Front, the He 111 participated in the *Barbarossa* campaign and during the bombardment of Stalingrad. During the air war, the He 111 also doubled as an impromptu transport—evacuating German troops from the Demyansk Pocket. Its effectiveness, however, waned in proportion to the decline of aerial bombardment within the Luftwaffe. By 1944, the plane itself had become obsolete and production ended in September of that year, as the Nazi high command halted bomber production in favor of fighter aircraft. By 1945, as the Luftwaffe's bomber force was practically defunct, the He 111 once again found itself conducting logistical missions.

Production of the He 111 continued after the war under license with the Spanish Air Force. Under a 1943 agreement, the Spanish company Construcciones Aeronáuticas SA, built a near-duplicate of the He 111: the CASA 2.111. The latter-day Spanish variant remained in service until the mid-1950s.

A pair of Heinkel He 111s stands on the tarmac before launching on another mission. The He 111 was among the best-recognized German bombers of World War II. Despite its weak defensive armament, it remained one of the most reliable and casualty-producing weapons of the war.

In Profile:
Fw 190A-9 and He 111

The Focke-Wulf Fw 190A-9. Although the Bf 109 held the crown in the Luftwaffe's fighter units, the Fw 190 was, in many respects, a superior fighter. Fast and highly maneuverable, the Focke Wulf packed a deadly punch as a fighter and later as a ground-attack aircraft.

Heinkel's He 111 was among the most recognizable aircraft in the Luftwaffe's bomber fleet. Pictured here is the H-16 variant. Along the Eastern Front, the He 111 was a frequent sight over Soviet cities and Red Army troop formations.

A Junkers Ju 88 from KG 77 in flight near the Mediterranean. A distant cousin to the Ju 87, the Ju 88 was a heavier bomber that was adapted to a variety of aerial roles along every front where it was stationed. Its adaptive roles included dive-bomber, torpedo-bomber, and night-fighter.

Junkers Ju 88

Distant cousin to the Ju 87 Stuka was the Junkers Ju 88. A twin-engine, multirole aircraft, the Ju 88 was designed almost in parallel to the Stuka. While the Ju 87 was designed as a dive-bomber, the Ju 88 was conceived as a "fast bomber"—a tactical bomber that could outrun enemy fighters and interceptors. Despite a tumultuous design and prototype process, the Ju 88 became one of the most versatile combat aircraft of the war—serving as a bomber, dive-bomber, torpedo-bomber, and night fighter.

From 1936 to 1945, more than 15,000 Ju 88s were built—making it the highest-produced twin-engine aircraft of the Luftwaffe. Along the Eastern Front, the Ju 88 flew alongside the He 111 and the Dornier Do 17, a less-renowned but still reliable bomber.

Dornier Do 17

The Dornier Do 17 was the last of the three primary bombers used by the Luftwaffe during the early years of World War II. A light bomber by design, it was often referred to as the *Fliegender Bleistift* (literally: "flying pencil"). The Do 17 was produced by Dornier Flugzeugwerke and, like the Ju 88, it was intended to be a "fast bomber", a bomber capable of outrunning enemy fighters and interceptors.

Designed in the early 1930s, the Do 17 made its combat debut during the Spanish Civil War, operating alongside the Ju 87 and He 111 as part of the Condor Legion. The Dornier featured prominently during the blitzkrieg and in the opening stages of the Eastern Front. However, as Soviet forces penetrated deeper into the Soviet homeland, use of the Do 17 trailed off as its payload capacity and flight range were limited.

The Do 17 featured two engines mounted on a "shoulder wing" structure and sported double tailfins. The combined structure made the Do 17 highly maneuverable for a bomber, especially at lower altitudes, thus making it a harder target for Allied bandits and air defense crewmen. The forward fuselage, in many ways, resembled the He 111, with its fully glazed nose. The "flying pencil" moniker described many of the early variants as its silhouette was rather stick-like.

The Do 17 typically carried a crew of four: the pilot, bombardier, and two gunners. As with many German bombers of the day, the crew sat within a single compartment. Aside from its payload bombs, the Do 17's defensive armaments included multiple MG 15 machine guns. The standard load for the secondary armaments was 3,300 rounds of 7.92mm ammunition.

The fuselage of the "flying pencil" was nearly 52 feet long. Aside from its handling, the narrow fuselage presented a narrower target to the enemy, thus creating a passive survivability feature. Another passive safety feature was its self-sealing fuel tanks, thus reducing the loss of fuel and risk of catastrophic explosions if the plane was hit in action. Oxygen bottles were also provided to crewmen for long flights above 12,000 feet.

The Do 17 was powered by a Bramo 323 A-1 powerplant. This engine meant that the Do 17 could only reach a top speed of 219 miles per hour, slower than what was needed to make it a qualitatively "fast bomber." The fuel mileage also ensured that the Do 17 could travel at ranges of only 400 nautical miles. Later variants of the Do 17 were equipped with improved Bramo 323P, which increased the plane's overall performance.

Although the Do 17 featured prominently during the first three years of World War II, its production ended in 1940, making way for the more powerful Junkers Ju 88. When production of the Do 17 ended, Dornier began development of the Do 217, which served predominantly in Western Europe and the Mediterranean. Even with the development of the 217, the Do 17 continued in service until the end of the war. Only a handful of Do 17s survived the war, the last being scrapped in Finland in 1952. In 2013, however, a British salvaging team successfully raised the remains of a Dornier Do 17Z buried in the seabed off the coast of Kent, England.

Although not as renowned as the He 111, the Dornier Do 17 was nevertheless a formidable bomber on the Eastern Front. The Do 17 was designed as a "fast bomber"—built to outrun any enemy fighter in the sky. Due to its unusual design, crewmen often referred to it as the "Flying Pencil."

Junkers Ju 52

Although it never had the panache of its stablemates—the Ju 87 and Ju 88—the Ju 52 was one of the most resilient aircraft of the Nazi regime. Entering service in 1930, it was also one of the oldest planes in the Luftwaffe's inventory. In fact, it had been designed as a commercial transport, and it flew with multiple airlines, including Swissair and Lufthansa. After the onset of the Third Reich, however, the Ju 52 was pressed into service with the Luftwaffe, where it deployed nearly everywhere the Wehrmacht had troops.

A Junkers Ju 52 at an airfield in Finland. Rounding out the Junkers wartime inventory was the Ju 52. The Ju 52 predated both World War II and the Nazi regime. Created as a civil transport, it found new life as a troop-carrier during the war and was hailed for its resilience in evacuating the beleaguered German troops following the battle of Moscow.

During its military service, the Ju 52 was primarily a troop and cargo transport, although it was briefly used as a medium bomber. The Ju 52 was unique among the early Luftwaffe planes due to its tri-mounted motors. Originally powered by three Pratt & Whitney R-1690 Hornet engines, later models used the BMW 132 engine. The Ju 52 was also built with a corrugated duralumin metal outer-skin (considered a novelty at the time), which strengthened the overall airframe and provided smoother aerodynamics. Its landing gear, however, was fixed—the Ju 52 variants could be equipped with wheels, skids, or pontoons depending on operational needs.

Unlike other Nazi-era aircraft, the Ju 52 had a long post-war service life—flying in various militaries and civilian organizations into the 1980s. Even today in the 21st century, several Ju 52s remain operational, where they perform in airshows or act as regional transports.

| Operation *Barbarossa*

By mid-1941, the Axis Powers had dominated Western Europe (save Great Britain) and had a comfortable foothold in the Balkans and North Africa. German expansion, and its attendant blitzkrieg, however, had left the Reich in dire need of raw materials, thus prompting Hitler to eye the mineral-rich Soviet Union. As early as December 1940, Hitler had begun making preparations for an invasion of the USSR—evaluating potential strengths and weaknesses of the Soviet air and ground forces.

Although Russia was territorially vast, Hitler concluded that (a) the Soviet infrastructure was weak, and (b) its military had been atrophied by the Great Purge. At the same time, Hitler knew that a protracted war in Russia could be disastrous—thus, a quick victory would be essential. The plan, therefore, would be to push as far east as the Ural Mountains, capturing the heart of Soviet industry and enveloping the capital, Moscow.

Although still reeling from its defeat in the battle of Britain, the Luftwaffe was ready for action in the spring of 1941, and played a vital role in the opening stages of the German advance. Indeed, nearly 65 percent of the Luftwaffe's forces were deployed in support of Operation *Barbarossa*. For the aerial campaign, the plan was simple: the Luftwaffe would provide operational-level air interdiction in support of rapid ground advances, running close air support as needed. The primary missions included targeting enemy air bases, logistics, and lines of communication. Hitler initially forbade any air strikes on Soviet factories or other places of industry—his intent was to conquer the Soviet Union, not destroy it. Hitler needed the industrial heartland to remain intact if he were to convert it to Axis use. However, in order for this "eastern blitzkrieg" to work, the Luftwaffe would have to eliminate the Red Air Force before it could take to the air to defend the homeland skies.

A destroyed MiG-3 sits on what remains of the Soviet airfield near Białystok. During the opening rounds of Operation *Barbarossa*, much of the Red Air Force in western Russia was destroyed before it even got off the ground.

Another destroyed MiG-3 is inspected by German troops, August 1941.

From the start, it seemed that the Luftwaffe had the upper hand. Their air–ground coordination was the best in the world. Every mechanized and panzer division had a cadre of forward air controllers attached to it. Despite the attrition of personnel suffered during the battle of Britain, the Luftwaffe still had an experienced and highly proficient corps of officers and support personnel. Despite this organizational strength, however, the Luftwaffe had paid virtually no attention to logistics when planning for *Barbarossa*—a mistake that would cost them dearly.

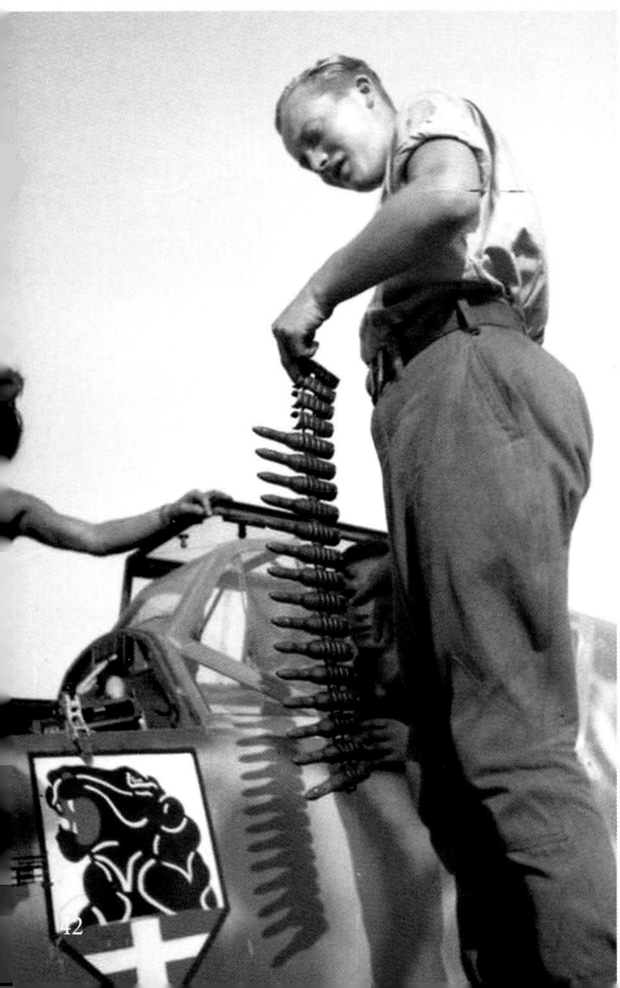

A German airman loads ammunition into a Bf 109 belonging to JG 54, forward-stationed along the Eastern Front, August 1941.

By comparison, the Red Air Force, although still recovering from Stalin's purges, was not as ill-equipped as the Wehrmacht believed. In fact, the technological quality of its fighter aircraft was close to that of the Luftwaffe's. The Yak-1, for example, could hold its own against a Bf 109E, but the MiG-3 and the early Lavochkin fighters were slower and clumsier. At the start of *Barbarossa*, the western contingent of the Red Air Force had more than 7,800 aircraft, and had a far better operational rate than the German intelligence community had anticipated. To make matters worse, the Luftwaffe ignored the input of its own envoys to the Red Air Force.

For example, Heinrich Aschenbrenner had been the Luftwaffe's attaché to Moscow, and was one of the few German officers with real-time knowledge of the

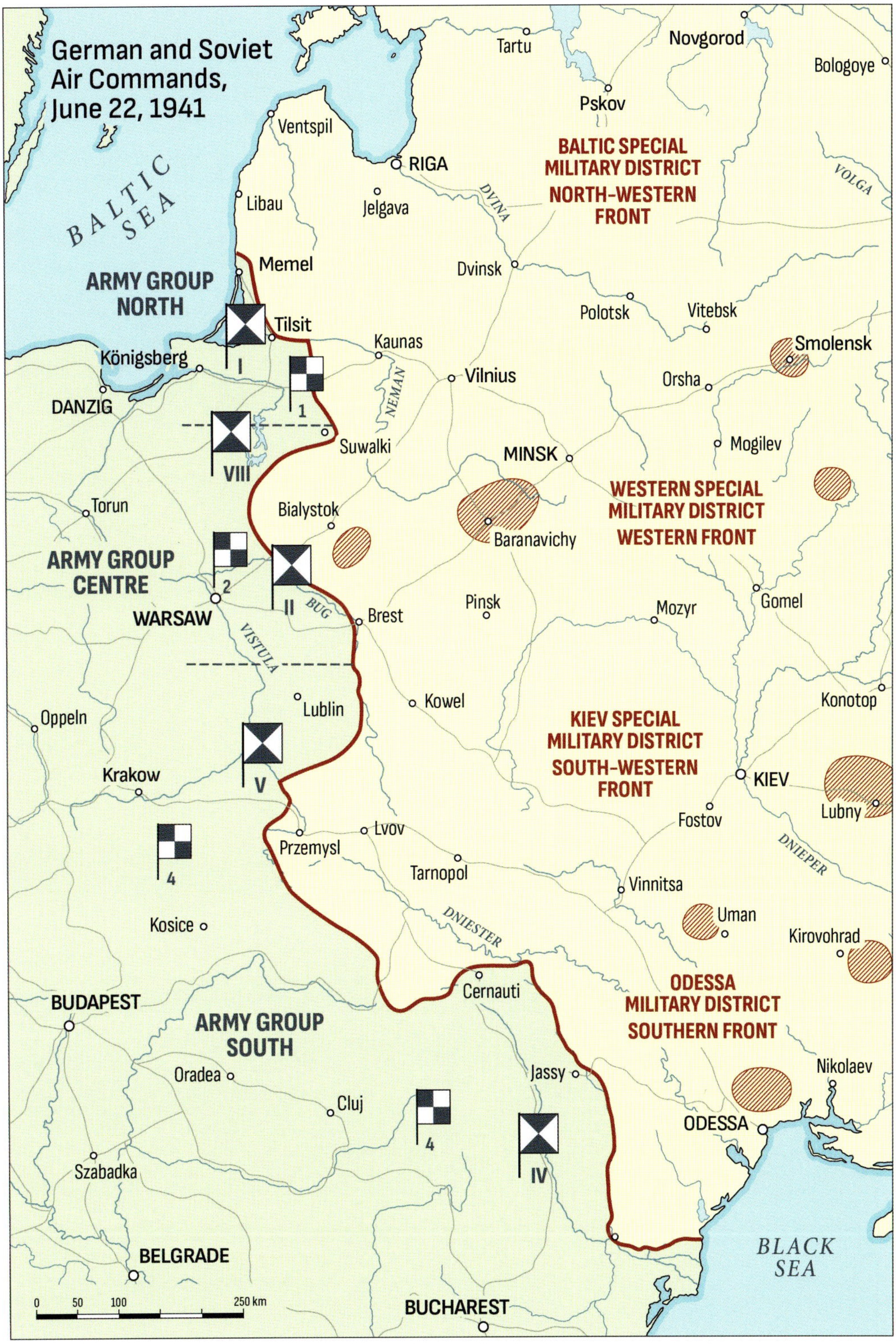

The disposition of the Luftwaffe's expeditionary forces on the eve of Operation *Barbarossa*, the German invasion of the Soviet Union. The combined forces were sufficient to penetrate deep into the Soviet homeland, but as the harsh Russian winter descended upon the Luftwaffe (and the Soviets began rolling back Nazi forces), the Luftwaffe had to divert many of its assets from the North African theater.

During a break in operations, this German crew conducts maintenance on a Bf 109, to include boresighting the plane's 20mm cannon.

Jubilant German soldiers pose atop the wreckage of a Polikarpov I-16 fighter in the summer of 1941. Built in the early 1930s, the I-16 was the first Soviet fighter to have retractable landing gear and armored plating to protect the pilot.

A crash-landed Yak-1 on the Eastern Front. Although the Red Air Force took valiantly to the sky to defend the Soviet homeland, their initial forays against the Luftwaffe were often unsuccessful.

In what became a recurring episode during Operation *Barbarossa*, a destroyed MiG-3 lies in shattered silence along the Russian steppes. Having just come into service in 1941, the MiG-3 was little match for the Bf 109 at low and medium altitudes. In terms of percentages, MiG-3 losses were higher than other Soviet aircraft of the day.

A German soldier poses proudly against the background of a downed MiG-3 in the summer of 1941.

Downed Ilyushin Il-2s in Western Russia. Although deadly as a ground-attack aircraft, the Il-2 was ill-suited as a fighter. Shturmovik pilots often found themselves doubling as fighter pilots due to the shortage of available fighter aircraft. In this role, however, the Shturmovik was easily outclassed by the Bf 109 and Fw 190.

Red Air Force's capabilities. In the spring of 1941, he had visited a series of aircraft plants in the Ural Mountains, and informed the Nazi regime of Soviet armaments potential, and their ability to carry on production within the Ural landscape. Aschenbrenner's input and analysis, however, were ignored. Indeed, the German view of Soviet airpower was still tainted by the Red Air Force's poor performance during the Spanish Civil War and the Winter War with Finland.

For the morning of the attack, June 22, 1941, Hitler ordered the Luftwaffe to attack Soviet airfields at dawn. Flying under limited visibility, the inaugural Luftwaffe task forces targeted Soviet redoubts in the western borderlands, hitting the fighter bases first, thereby crippling any potential opposition to the first wave of German aircraft.

These attacks began at 3 a.m. on June 22. Despite warnings from his most trusted intelligence sources, Stalin had dismissed the idea that an attack from Nazi Germany was imminent. As a result, the Red Air Force was grossly unprepared for the onslaught of Hitler's Luftwaffe. Not expecting an attack, the Soviets had clustered their aircraft together into neat rows, rendering them prime targets for Axis bombers. The results were catastrophic.

For example, at the Pinsk airfield, the 39th Mixed Bomber Aviation Regiment lost 48 bombers (43 SBs and five Pe-2s) on the ground after being strafed by the Dornier Do 17s

The Il-2 sports its twin-mounted 37mm cannons. This deadly armament proved highly effective against German armor.

and Junkers Ju 88s of Kampfgeschwader 3. Farther west, the 33rd Fighter Aviation Regiment lost 46 of its prized Polikarpov I-16s and I-153s to the Messerschmitts of Jagdgeschwader 51. Meanwhile, the Soviets lost an additional 50 aircraft at Korbin, near the headquarters of the Soviet 4th Army. Within hours, the Red Air Force had lost an additional 100 aircraft before they even got airborne.

Although shocked by the sudden onslaught, the Red Air Force was quick to respond. Indeed, the Soviets flew nearly 6,000 sorties on the first day of the air war. It was during these opening volleys that the Luftwaffe realized how fierce and determined the Soviet flyers could be. Such was their intensity that they seemed to be unfazed by their losses. At several points along the burgeoning air front, Soviet pilots were literally *ramming* German planes, in a style reminiscent of the Japanese kamikaze.

The charred remains of a Pe-2 bomber, downed by the Luftwaffe, 1941.

Stalin and the Soviet high command, meanwhile, were stunned by the invasion, and indeed it took them several hours to process what was happening. On his order, he scrambled every available Soviet bomber into the air. Having lost many of their frontier fighters, however, these bombers took to the sky without escort. Unprotected from the likes of the Bf 109, the Soviet bombers suffered devastating losses—sometimes flying, literally, to the last surviving crewman. Despite these losses, however, the Red Air Force bombers kept coming—showing a tenacity that shocked even the most seasoned German pilots.

By the end of the first day, the Germans reported nearly 1,500 Soviet aircraft destroyed on the ground. In reality, however, the figure was closer to 2,500. The initial devastation surprised even Hermann Göring—who, at first, refused to believe that the Luftwaffe had made such short work of the Soviet airfields. In fact, entire units were nearly wiped out. The 9th Mixed Aviation Division, for example, lost 347 out of 409 aircraft—including most of its MiG-3s. The division commander, Sergey Chernykh, was executed for the perceived failure.

Still, the Soviets were putting up a tremendous fight against the Wehrmacht. Relative to their size, Axis losses were staggering. The Luftwaffe's tally for aircraft lost on June 22 totaled 78. In all, the Germans lost 24 Bf 109s, seven Bf 110s, 11 He 111s, two Ju 87s, one Do 17, and 10 additional aircraft of miscellaneous types.

During the first week of the campaign, as the Red Air Force limped its way into the air against the Luftwaffe, the Red Army thrust itself against the German Army on the ground. Along the Soviets' Northwestern Front (i.e. the Baltic Military District) the Red Army's 3rd, 12th, and 23rd Mechanized Corps counterattacked German Army Group North. From the air, however, KG 76 and KG 77 from Luftflotte 1 inflicted heavy losses on all three mechanized units. At one point, the Soviet 12th Mechanized Corps lost 40 combat vehicles to the Luftwaffe's bombardment. Meanwhile, the unescorted Soviet bombers continued, in vain, to disrupt the Luftwaffe's advance. In sending their bombers aloft unescorted, the Red Air Force contributed to its own demise—since Soviet fighters were kept on a tight leash to safeguard the industrial cities, the vulnerable bombers were torn from the sky by opportunistic German fighters.

On the ground, the Red Army appeared to be performing comparatively better, although they were still losing ground to the Wehrmacht. Entire Soviet armies were being encircled, but the German ground forces had trouble maintaining these pockets once the

A flight of Fw 190s prepares for action. One advantage of the Focke-Wulf was its wide-track undercarriage, making it highly adaptable to the rough airfields along the Eastern Front.

In Profile:
Sturzkampfgeschwader 77

A pair of Stukas from II./StG 77 position themselves into a second dive over their targets. To the left, the bombs from their first dive have already detonated in a spectacular explosion. The two dots seen above the Stukas are Soviet armored vehicles that have broken ranks from their convoy. According to the pilots, both Soviet vehicles were destroyed during this mission.

A Junkers Ju 87 Stuka dive-bomber in flight. During the early days of World War II, the Stuka garnered a fearsome reputation due largely to its dive-activated air siren. It played a critical role in the bombing campaigns along the Eastern Front, but its poor maneuverability made it easy prey for Allied fighters.

Flying the Ju 87 Stuka, Sturzkampfgeschwader 77 (StG 77) served with distinction during the blitzkrieg, the Battle of Britain, and along the Eastern Front. In the skies over Soviet Russia, StG 77 fought at the battle of Stalingrad and provided close air support to Wehrmacht ground units at Kursk. However, StG 77's performance suffered as the Stuka's effectiveness waned. Because the Ju 87 was primarily a dive-bomber aircraft, it fared poorly in air-to-air combat against the ever-improving Soviet fighters. To make matters worse, as the war dragged on, the Luftwaffe could no longer spare adequate numbers of Bf 109s to accompany the Stukas into battle. Thus, in October 1943, the Stuka units were reorganized and integrated into fighter-bomber units spearheaded by the Focke-Wulf Fw 190. On October 18, 1943, Sturzkampfgeschwader 77 (StG 77) thus became Schlachtgeschwader 77 (SG 77), reflecting its new role as ground-attack unit instead of a pure dive-bombing unit.

A Dornier Do 17 in action. Although a formidable bomber in its own right, the Do 17 had been rendered obsolete by the dawn of 1942. It saw considerable service during *Barbarossa*, but was largely withdrawn from frontline service after 1941.

Along the Eastern Front, one of the He 111's primary roles was that of a "train buster"—an attack aircraft dedicated to targeting the Soviet Union's vast rail network. The He 111, however, could not operate effectively without a fighter escort. It also doubled as a transport and cargo plane until the end of the war.

A Ju 88 in flight. One of the most versatile aircraft in the Luftwaffe, the Ju 88 was also one of the most mass-produced, totaling nearly 15,000 units built.

During a break in operations, this Ju 88 flight crew takes a moment to enjoy a leisurely game of cards on the Eastern Front.

A close-up view of the Ju 88's forward crew compartment. Depending on its variant, the Ju 88 could accommodate a crew of up to four.

The charred remains of Soviet fighters give mute testimony to the destruction that much of the Red Air Force suffered before it could get under way during Operation *Barbarossa*.

A Lend-Lease P-39 Airacobra in Soviet service. Before and after America's entry into World War II, the US donated significant amounts of military equipment to the Soviet Union under the auspices of the Lend-Lease program. Although the P-39 was not well liked by American pilots, the Soviet airmen adored it. Indeed, while in Soviet service, the P-39 was among the most successful planes of the Red Air Force.

Red Air Force Commander A. A. Osipov discusses aerial strike tactics with a group of young P-39 pilots, 1943.

encirclements were complete. Indeed, the Red Army often broke out at night. To prevent further Soviet breakouts, Luftflotte 2 began flying armed reconnaissance missions, using bombers to suppress the Soviet ground forces. Unwittingly, the Red Army made the encirclement easier for the Germans because the former hadn't integrated radios into their command and control formations—relying instead on telephone lines, most of which had been damaged by air attacks. Nevertheless, Soviet ground units were ordered to fire all available weapons at the Luftwaffe's close air support planes. This virtual "wall of steel" inflicted heavy losses on the Germans' frontline aerial fleets. Indeed, by June 28, the Luftwaffe, although still commanding the skies, had cut its number of sorties in half.

A Lend-Lease Hawker Hurricane lies crash-landed near Kestenga, March 1942. The British government was another contributor to the Red Air Force, donating over 7,000 Hawker Hurricanes, Supermarine Spitfires, de Havilland Mosquitos and other aircraft.

As the Germans closed in on Minsk, the remaining Red Air Force units in Western Russia made an all-out effort to stop the Axis advance. The 3rd Bomber Aviation Corps, the 42nd, 47th, and 52nd Aviation Divisions, along with the 1st and 3rd Heavy Bomber Aviation Regiments, attacked German positions near Bobruysk, attempting to prevent the enemy from crossing the Berezina River. The result, however, was a disaster for the Red Air Force.

German fighter and anti-aircraft units devastated the Soviet bomber formations. According to German sources, the Soviets lost 146 aircraft during this engagement alone.

The destroyed remains of a Soviet air base, June 1941. On the first day of Operation *Barbarossa*, at least 66 Soviet airfields were struck by the Luftwaffe.

Although bridges were difficult targets for the Ju 87 Stuka to destroy, bridges along the Eastern Front featured heavily on the Stukas' target list. With the Stuka, Ju 88, and He 111, the Luftwaffe targeted several bridges between Warsaw and Moscow to trap and destroy the Soviet forces.

June 22, 1941 – the widespread destruction of Soviet planes on the ground continues.

The twisted wreckage of an I-153 fighter lingers in the foreground of a captured Soviet air base. The speed of the German advance into the Soviet Union stunned both the Axis and Allies. Within months, the Germans were within striking distance of Moscow.

Once the Red Air Force had been neutralized, the Luftwaffe set its sights squarely on the Red Army. Taking punishment from the Ju 87s and Do 17s, the Red Army troops were soon on the run and, in many places, trapped within a series of pockets in Byelorussia and Ukraine. In this photograph, the crew of this vehicle futilely sought shelter underneath it.

Dead Soviet infantrymen, victims of the Luftwaffe's strafing attacks during *Barbarossa*.

By July 1, the western contingent of the Red Air Force could only muster about 500 aircraft—down from nearly 1,800 just 10 days earlier.

All told, June 1941 was a catastrophe for the Red Air Force. The Luftwaffe owned the skies, and the Soviet counterattacks were having little effect. The silver lining, however, appeared to be the Ilyushin Il-2, a rugged ground-attack aircraft that seemed impervious to enemy fire. Indeed, the German fighters who had interdicted the Soviets' 4th Attack Aviation Regiment, marveled at the Il-2's heavy armor, which effortlessly deflected fire from the Bf 109s' onboard cannons.

The Red Air Force's initial defeats were attributed to (a) the lack of communication between Soviet pilots, and (b) the better tactics of the Luftwaffe. The Luftwaffe's two-plane Rotte formations operated on the wingman–leader concept, flying 200 meters apart and covering each other's blind spots. In combat, the leader engaged while the wingman covered the leader. Soviet aircraft, on the other hand, flew with little regard for tactical formations. The lack of cockpit radios in the Soviet aircraft, understandably, made the situation worse.

The second month of *Barbarossa*, July 1941, wasn't much better for Stalin's airmen. By mid-month, the western contingent of the Red Air Force had been all but destroyed. German pilots reported more than 1,000 aerial victories. That month, bombers from the Luftwaffe's KG 1, KG 76, and KG 77 disrupted Soviet communication lines, slowing down the Red Army and allowing the panzer divisions to blaze forward. On July 5, the Red Air Force mounted another counterattack, but the Luftwaffe quickly repelled it, destroying another 112 Soviet

He 111s fly into action for a bombing run over Moscow, July 1941. Although the German ground forces had yet to encroach the Soviet capital, the Luftwaffe was eager to begin its bombardment of the city and the surrounding area. All seemed poised for success until the unexpectedly harsh winter descended upon the Wehrmacht.

A German crewman paints a winter camouflage pattern on the wings of a Ju 87 for service along the Eastern Front. Several other German aircraft received these paint conversions.

aircraft on the ground. Soviet ground forces, meanwhile, counterattacked and destroyed an advance party of the 1st Panzer Division. Still, the three bomber groups interdicted, flying ground support missions at Ostrov, and destroying 140 Soviet tanks.

Despite these continuing setbacks, the Red Air Force was starting to emerge from its initial shock and atrophy. On July 7, for example, the Red Air Force slowed the Germans' advance and effectively stopped the 4th Panzer Army's advance on Leningrad. By the second week in July, Soviet airmen had flown more than 1,000 sorties, dropping some 500 tons of ordnance. Within the Wehrmacht's Army Group North, losses in equipment and personnel were heavy, especially for the 1st and 6th Panzer Divisions. Almost simultaneously, the Soviet bomber units began reevaluating their tactics. Going forward, all bomber formations would fly under fighter escort. Soviet fighter pilots, meanwhile, were encouraged to be more aggressive and begin flying low-level suppression attacks, while conducting more night missions. These and other reassessments helped increase the effectiveness of the struggling Red Air Force.

July 1941 also highlighted the emerging effectiveness of the Ilyushin Il-2 Shturmovik. On July 5, for example, as the Luftwaffe supported the drive into Smolensk, the Soviet 46th Mixed Aviation Division, with its spearhead force of Il-2s, poured in to stop the German advance. One Il-2, piloted by Nikolai Malyshev, of the 46th Division's 430th Attack Aviation Regiment, sustained 200 hits to his aircraft, yet remained aloft. Although the Soviets lagged behind in the game of attrition, their dogged persistence was beginning to wear down the momentum of the German advance. By the end of the month, Army Group North had failed to capture Leningrad or destroy the Red Army's North-Western Front. Also, the Luftwaffe was beginning to run into logistical problems of its own.

By the end of July, the biggest problem facing the Axis was its dwindling number of available aircraft. Because the Luftwaffe was spread thin from North Africa to Central Europe,

Il-2 Shturmoviks in flight over Nazi positions near Moscow.

they could not budget enough airframes to sustain the momentum behind *Barbarossa*. The Soviets' industrial base, meanwhile, continued to focus its resources and manpower in stemming the tide of fascist expansionism. As Soviet factories continued working at breakneck speed, the Red Air Force received 900 new aircraft in July 1941. Meanwhile, the Luftwaffe along the Eastern Front was falling to half of its original strength. Adding to the Soviets' increased fortune was their receipt of hundreds of Lend-Lease aircraft from Great Britain and the United States. Planes such as the Hawker Hurricane and the P-39 Airacobra flew alongside the domestically built MiGs and Illuyshins as the Red Air Force stubbornly persisted in its efforts to halt the Nazis' advance.

Another factor in the Soviets' reversal of fortune was the very size of their homeland. The vastness of the Soviet Union strained even the best of the Luftwaffe's support units. In fact, these long distances had begun to take their toll on the Führer's fighter squadrons. Although the Germans still had superior aircraft and combat tactics, their planes were tethered to a logistical leash that prevented them from flying farther and staying aloft longer. By the end of the summer, the Luftwaffe could only establish air superiority on a local basis—wherever they had the highest concentration of Bf 109s. By now, even the German ground forces had begun complaining about Soviet air superiority. From these developments, it was clear that the air supremacy won by the Luftwaffe during the initial forays was beginning to slip away.

To effect its deceleration of the German advance, the Red Air Force transferred large quantities of aircraft from all over the Soviet Union, including many that were obsolete or had been training aircraft. This influx of equipment brought the Red Air Force to a

Anti-aircraft gunners on the roof of the Moskva Hotel. As the Germans closed in on the Soviet capital, the Red Army and Red Air Force rallied to beat back the enemy advance. Almost simultaneously, Soviet citizens took to the streets to defend their capital city.

The Soviets barricaded the streets of their capital, making ready for the German advance on Moscow.

Soviet technicians prepare to launch a barrage balloon over Moscow. Barrage balloons were shaped like dirigibles and tethered to steel cables, to act as barriers to incoming aircraft, and increasing the risk of mid-air collisions.

Soviet citizens make a proud and somewhat mocking display of a downed German Ju 88 in Moscow. Although the Soviet citizenry had suffered under years of heavy-handed Stalinist rule, they nevertheless rallied to expel the Nazis from the Motherland.

German soldiers marching into captivity on a snow-covered field near Moscow, 1942. The harsh Russian winters were beyond anything the Wehrmacht had expected. Ill-prepared for the double-digit subzero temperatures, their equipment and morale suffered, while the Soviets regained the initiative.

A Ju 87 prepares for another bombing raid against Soviet positions, March 1942.

strength of 3,700 aircraft by August. Unfortunately, most of their aircrews were ill-trained and inexperienced, thus continuing the trend of heavy losses for the Soviet military. And although the Red Air Force had not yet halted the German ground forces, they were nevertheless exacting a heavy toll on the Luftwaffe. The Soviets' handiwork was most evident in the number of losses sustained by German transport units. Such was the intensity of the air battle over Smolensk, that Hitler shifted his attention to Leningrad.

Late summer 1941 was a critical point in the course of events for *Barbarossa*. The Wehrmacht had shifted its attention northward to Leningrad and south to Kiev. This led many within the Soviet Union (civilian and military) to believe that the German advance had been halted short of Moscow. In reality, however, the Wehrmacht was trying to envelop the Eastern Front and isolate the capital region.

The battle for Leningrad, in the air and on the ground, precipitated the largest siege in modern history. In accordance with Hitler's new directive, the Luftwaffe moved Fliegerkorps VIII from Luftflotte 2 to Luftflotte 1, giving the latter its much-needed ground support units. The new Fliegerkorps units thus included a variety of Do 17s and Ju 87s. On August 8, 1941, the 4th Panzer Army began its initial assault southwest of Leningrad. To keep the Wehrmacht at bay, General Markian Popov, commander of the Red Army's Northwestern Front, ordered all available Soviet air forces to interdict the Axis advance. When the weather cleared on August 10, the 2nd Bomber Aviation Division and 7th Fighter Aviation Regiment of the 5th Mixed Aviation Division took to the air to interdict the Germans' advance on Leningrad. During that engagement, Il-2s from the 288th Attack Aviation Regiment scored

As the Germans attempted to flee the Moscow front in early 1942, the Junkers Ju 52 became an unlikely savior, ferrying supplies to beleaguered comrades and acting as an impromptu medevac plane.

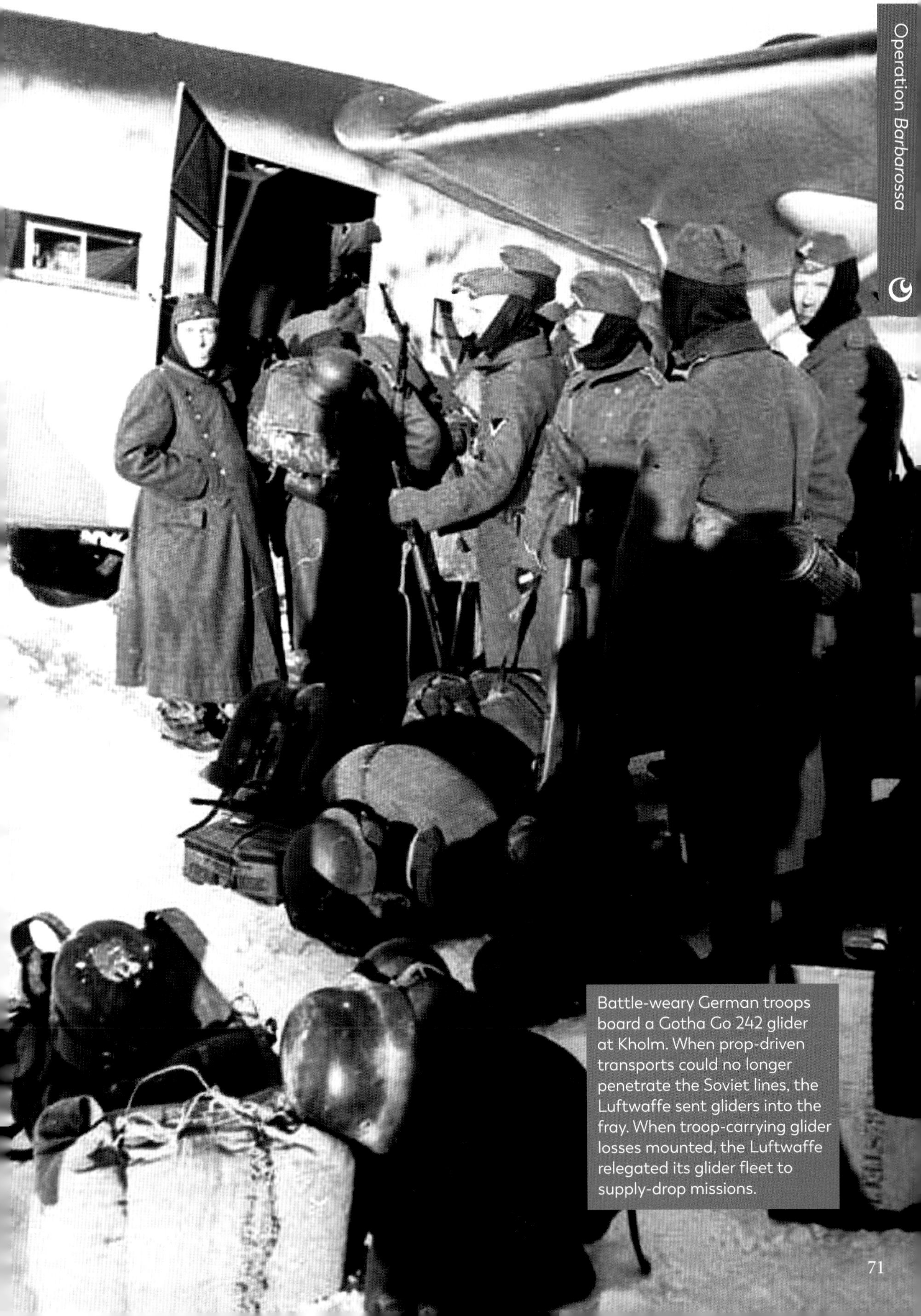

Battle-weary German troops board a Gotha Go 242 glider at Kholm. When prop-driven transports could no longer penetrate the Soviet lines, the Luftwaffe sent gliders into the fray. When troop-carrying glider losses mounted, the Luftwaffe relegated its glider fleet to supply-drop missions.

A Ju 52 camouflaged for winter operations arrives at Demyansk, 1942.

numerous hits against Axis ground forces—a representative victory of the 908 sorties flown by the Red Air Force that day. Luftflotte 1, meanwhile, flew 1,126 sorties—claiming 210 ground vehicle kills and 15 artillery pieces.

By August 13, the German 11th Army had reached Lake Novgorod and its namesake city, enabling the Wehrmacht to cut communication between Moscow and Leningrad. The ensuing battle in and around Novgorod lasted 11 days, with the Stukas from StG 2 playing a vital role in destroying supply bridges and the fortress within the city itself. Although Novgorod proper was abandoned on August 24, local contingents of the Red Army and Red Air Force poured into the area and counterattacked near Staraya Russa. The Luftwaffe responded by throwing all of Fliegerkorps VIII into the melee against the Soviet formations. The German bomber units, including I./KG 4, conducted a series of rolling attacks over the Soviet front, all of which had a devastating effect on the Soviet positions. The Do 17s from KG 2, for example, destroyed 18 Soviet tanks during one mission.

By the end of August, the Germans were inching closer to Leningrad, but there was little doubt that the Red Army and the Red Air Force had hindered the speed of the Axis advance. As the German panzer forces tried to encircle the Soviets in the Luga–Novgorod area, the Red Air Force responded by sending in the 6th and 402d Fighter Aviation Regiments, reviving Soviet air power along that section of the Eastern Front. Equipped with 32 new LaGG-3 fighters, these newly arrived aviation regiments came to the battlefront with a combined strength of 174 aircraft.

In the air battles that followed, the German pilots reluctantly acknowledged that the Red Air Force had come back stronger. Although the XXXXI Panzerkorps succeeded in surrounding the Soviets in the Luga–Novgorod area, the Soviet 7th Fighter Aviation Corps engaged Fliegerkorps VIII in a series of air battles during the last week of August. In the ensuing aerial combat, the 7th Fighter Aviation Corps confirmed 25 kills, while acknowledging 44 losses. Although the Luftwaffe had numerically downed more planes, the double-digit kill record for the Soviet fighters was an unqualified morale booster for the Red Air Force.

By early September 1941, the Germans had completed their encirclement of Novgorod, capturing 20,000 Soviet troops. With Novgorod now in Axis hands, Army Group North began operations against Leningrad. On September 6, Fliegerkorps I and VIII began their aerial attacks with a relentless fury. It was, by all accounts, the most intense aerial bombardment to that point in history. Indeed, the two German air corps carried out more than 1,000 sorties during the first day of the assault on Leningrad. Of these, more than 180 sorties were concentrated on a front measuring less than 16 square miles. By concentrating two air corps onto the entire Leningrad sector, the Germans had achieved numerical superiority—mustering 481 aircraft against the Red Air Force's 286 (of which only 163 were operational).

A specially modified Ju 52 in its medical evacuation role. Throughout the winter of 1941/2, these Ju 52s successfully evacuated more than 22,000 wounded Germans from the Eastern Front.

On September 8, Army Group North initiated a two-pronged attack. Supporting the ground assault, Fliegerkorps VIII pounded the defending Soviet 54th Army, forcing it back from Lake Ladoga and cutting off Leningrad from potential reinforcements. The Luftwaffe's operations then shifted to the center of the city. On the night of September 8, the attendant Ju 88s dropped more than 6,000 pieces of ordnance, setting fire to 183 critical structures, including the strategic Badayevo warehouses. During this bombardment of Leningrad, the Luftwaffe flew mostly at night to avoid Soviet anti-aircraft fire. At this point, the Red Air Force was still lagging in its night-fighter capabilities.

On September 12, the local Red Air Force commander was ordered to dispatch all available aircraft against German troop concentrations near Leningrad. Despite heavy interdictions from Soviet fighter-bombers, however, the German 58th Infantry Division captured the district of Krasnoye Selo, well within the city limits of Leningrad. The following day, the Soviet high command pulled aircraft from various commands to provide relief to the beleaguered city. This relief force included utility aircraft from the Civil Air Fleet, along with six squadrons from the Moscow Air Group—three of which flew directly from Moscow to Leningrad. By the end of October, Soviet civil aviation was delivering 150 tons of supply to Leningrad daily. Throughout the early winter, these civil and liaison aircraft delivered more than 6,000 tons of food and ammunition to the city, flying more than 1,500 resupply missions escorted by Soviet fighters. Though effective in keeping the city resupplied, Leningrad would remain under siege from the Wehrmacht until January 1944—a total of 872 days.

Two Il-2 crewman pose on their Ilyushin Il-2, spring 1942. As the Soviets regained the initiative, the Il-2 "Flying Tank" became the spearhead of the 1942 counteroffensive, disrupting and destroying German ground units with a ferocity hitherto unseen by the Wehrmacht.

Although Leningrad remained under siege, the Red Army, Red Air Force, and the local populace made it excruciatingly difficult for the Wehrmacht to overtake the city. Fed up with the three-dimensional beatings from the Soviets, and now struck by logistical issues, Hitler decided to abandon the capture of Leningrad, content for now to maintain the siege while he turned his attention to Moscow.

To effect the drive to Moscow, Fliegerkorps I's III./KG 4 and KG 76 were reassigned to support Army Group Center. All of Fliegerkorps VIII, meanwhile, was diverted to the Moscow offensive. For their part, the Red Air Force along the northern fronts had been reduced to the size of a single division—with only 191 aircraft on hand by the end of September. Fortunately, Soviet intelligence had correctly determined that the Wehrmacht was shifting its focus from Leningrad to Moscow—thus prompting the Red Army and the Red Air Force to divert most of its assets for the defense of the capital.

Although the Luftwaffe had been bombing Moscow since the previous summer, the final assault on the Soviet capital proved to be a disaster for the Luftwaffe. Ironically, it seemed that Mother Nature was the biggest culprit in the Luftwaffe's defeat. During the second half of December, the temperature dropped to a record low of -44°F. The extreme temperatures effectively paralyzed the Luftwaffe for the rest of the season. Thus, the Red Air Force, operating closer to their own logistical lines and now flying from better-prepared bases, grew stronger in the air. During the last two months of 1941, Soviet airmen logged more than 15,000 sorties. Of particular note was the 6th Fighter Corps, which claimed to have downed 250 German planes during the same timespan.

Two Soviet technicians remove the wheel chocks from an Il-2 in preparation for its combat sortie, 1942.

In these rare color photographs, German soldiers inspect an abandoned Ilyushin Il-2. For the German ground troops, fewer Soviet planes commanded more respect than the Il-2.

A downed Il-2 near Budapest, Hungary 1942.

By January 4, 1942 the Red Air Force had cleared the skies over Moscow.

By the end of *Barbarossa*, the Wehrmacht had failed to achieve its ultimate goals—the defeat of the Soviet armed forces and the capture of Moscow. Although the Germans had succeeded in approaching the Soviet capital, both sides had suffered enormous losses. By December 1941, both the Luftwaffe and the Red Air Force had endured the most horrific attritional air war to that point in history. During these opening rounds of the Eastern Front campaign, the Soviets lost some 21,000 aircraft, and the Axis hadn't fared much better.

Conclusively, weather and geography had aided the Soviet Union in its struggle to stem the tide of the Nazi invasion. The fierce Russian winter had stalled the German offensive; meanwhile the heart of Soviet industry lay deep within the Urals, far out of reach of the Luftwaffe's medium bombers. With its factories relatively safe from Nazi bombardment, Soviet military production surged, far outpacing the Nazis and thus enabling the Red Air Force to replenish its battered aerial fleets. Yet it seems that Hitler's overconfidence was the true genesis of the Axis defeat during *Barbarossa*. He had grossly underestimated the Soviets' resolve and their industrial potential. Despite their own oppression under Stalinist rule, the Soviets rallied around their despot to drive the Nazis from Mother Russia.

Hungarian civilians inspect the wreckage of a looted Il-2 Shturmovik. Hungarian forces fought along the Axis Powers throughout World War II, officially joining the German camp in June 1941. For the first three years of the war, the Hungarian populace, by and large, continued to live their normal lives, while enjoying these displays of downed Allied aircraft. However, Hungarian life drastically changed after Soviet troops occupied the country in 1944.

Soviet Counteroffensives

Now in retreat following the battle of Moscow, the German Army was in a desperate struggle to survive. Although the Luftwaffe received hasty reinforcements, it seemed there was little that Hitler's airmen could do to improve the situation for their ground-based counterparts. Indeed, from January 21 until May 5, 1942, nearly 5,500 German troops were trapped in the Kholm Pocket, south of Leningrad. Meanwhile, a much larger German force had been surrounded at Demyansk.

Attempting to relieve the encircled troops, the Luftwaffe initially sent a fleet of DFS 230 and Gotha Go 242 cargo gliders. The glider method, however, was problematic because Soviet anti-aircraft batteries made it nearly impossible for the non-maneuverable gliders to deliver

Stukas over Stalingrad, October 1942. Although the Luftwaffe delivered heavy bombardments to Soviet ground forces during the battle, it was not enough to turn the tide in the Axis favor.

their goods. As glider losses mounted, the Luftwaffe began delivering supplies to Kholm via parachute. Meanwhile, at Demyansk, the situation for German ground troops was far worse. Four Soviet field armies had penetrated the frontlines of the German 16th Army, encircling six of its divisions and trapping nearly 100,000 troops.

Assessing the situation, the commander of Luftflotte I, Colonel-General Alfred Keller made an appeal to Colonel Fritz Morzik, chief of the Luftwaffe's air transport arm. "To ferry a quota of 300 tons to Demyansk," Keller said, "I need a standing force of at least 150 serviceable machines and we only have half that number. To double it, you will have to draw on other fronts and drain the homeland of all available machines." The available Transportgruppen (airlift groups) had nearly 220 aircraft available, but only a third were serviceable.

Keller accepted Morzik's help, but the former had little choice other than to send a request for every available aircraft to be diverted to the Eastern Front. One such unit was redeployed from the deserts of North Africa to the frozen plains of western Russia. The continuing problem for these and other Luftwaffe units along the Eastern Front, was the perennial subzero weather, sometimes reaching in excess of 40°F below zero.

In his discussions with Morzik, Keller added that, in order to operate the aerial fleets in winter, "I require mobile workshops, vehicles to warm up the aero-engines, and auxiliary starters." Keller's request was reasonable, but the shortage of ground crews meant that the pilots themselves often had to service their own planes. Moreover, the harsh winter climate took a heavier toll on the aircrafts' serviceability. Everything from fuel lines to radios were hampered by the extreme subzero temperatures. To make matters worse, the landing tires

As the situation in Stalingrad deteriorated for the Axis, lesser-known aircraft such as the Ju 290 long-range bomber were wrangled into the roles of emergency transport and relief.

were running flat due to the brittle, cracking rubber. Although hampered by personnel and logistical shortages, the Luftwaffe's transport units succeeded in delivering nearly 300 tons of equipment per day to the German ground troops.

The first flight of Ju 52s into Demyansk launched on February 20, 1942. Initially, the Luftwaffe hoped that low-level, smaller formations would escape detection from the Red Air Force or the PVO. However, even these small formations fell prey to Soviet fighters and ground-based air defense units. In fact, it was during these initial stages of the Soviet counteroffensive that their fighter units came into their own. To interdict the incoming Ju 52s, the PVO dispatched the 6th Fighter Corps. Equipped with MiG-3s, Yak-1s, and Lend-Lease Hawker Hurricanes, the Soviet airmen intercepted the Ju 52s with varying degrees of success—typically based on the comparative strength of the German fighter escorts.

Despite the constant harassment from Soviet flak guns and interceptors, the Luftwaffe transports succeeded in delivering 24,303 tons of supplies to the trapped German divisions from February–May 1942. In addition to ferrying supplies, these Junkers transports evacuated more than 22,000 wounded soldiers to the Reich. Collectively, the aerial resupply helped prevent the collapse of Army Group Center. And although the Luftwaffe considered their transport missions a "success," the victory had come at a considerable cost. Indeed, Hitler's airmen lost some 265 Ju 52s—taking with them the most experienced aircrews in Nazi Germany. Still, the demonstrable victory at Demyansk convinced Hitler that the Luftwaffe could rescue the German Army wherever it might be. This assumption, however, would cost him dearly when the Germans entered Stalingrad.

Winterized Ju 52s continue their relief efforts to the troops trapped at Demyansk. Ju 52 unit commanders discovered that they could not resupply an entire German field army at Stalingrad.

A German air defense gunner on the lookout for any Soviet planes on the horizon. Stalingrad was a critical turning point for the Axis on the Eastern Front. After the German offensive stalled at Moscow, the Wehrmacht was roundly defeated at Stalingrad. Thereafter the Soviets began pushing the Wehrmacht back towards the borders of the Reich.

The devastation of Stalingrad. The battle was the largest in military history and was marked by intense urban combat, with the opposing sides fighting house by house, and a number of civilians joining in the fight.

Stalingrad was the largest battle of World War II. Spanning from August 1942 to February 1943, it was a true "urban battle," marked by intense house-to-house fighting. By all accounts, the battle of Stalingrad was also the bloodiest in history—with nearly 2 million people killed, wounded, or captured.

Although reeling from their defeat at Moscow and stung by their encirclements elsewhere along the Eastern Front, the Germans rallied to assault Stalingrad on August 23, 1942. Spearheaded by the German 6th Army and elements of the 4th Panzer Army, the attack on Stalingrad was supported by intense bombing from the Luftwaffe.

Throughout September, Luftflotte 4 conducted more than 900 sorties per day. Determined to wear down the Red Army's resistance, Stukas from Luftflotte 4 spearheaded the aerial bombardment over the city—targeting points of industry including the Stalingrad Tractor Factory. Meanwhile, these air assaults wiped out entire Soviet regiments.

After the Germans faltered at Moscow, Stalingrad became a rallying point for both Axis and Allies on the Eastern Front. Stalingrad was the largest battle in military history. From the air, the Luftwaffe delivered the best of its tactical squadrons in an attempt to break the Soviets' resolve. Visible on the map are the Luftwaffe's operations in support of German ground forces, targeting critical points along the northern banks of the Volga River and south towards the Caspian Sea.

The aerial bombardment of Stalingrad was among the most intense of World War II.

The Luftwaffe dominated the skies over Stalingrad into November and, during the opening months of the battle, Soviet aerial resistance was mediocre at best. However, the situation was not as it seemed. Indeed, the ongoing air operations since June 1941 had worn down the Luftwaffe's vitality. For Luftflotte 4, its original strength of 1,155 operational aircraft fell to barely 550 by late 1942. During the same timeframe, the unit's daily sortie rate fell from 1,343 to 975. Overall, the Soviet counteroffensive along the Eastern Front had diluted much of the Luftwaffe's assets, especially as the Germans diverted more airframes away from North Africa and Western Europe. Although the Red Air Force remained qualitatively inferior, they had now reached numerical superiority.

From the outset of Stalingrad, the city's airspace was defended by the 102nd Fighter Aviation Division, consisting of 80 fighters, most of which were outdated and outgunned I-15s and I-16s. To compensate for his overmatched fighters, the 102nd's commander, General P.S. Stepanov, requested a regiment of Yakovlev Yak-1s. Answering the call, General Novikov, the chief planning and operations officer of the Red Air Force, sent a fighter regiment from Moscow equipped with Yak-7s and Yak-9s.

In many ways, Stalingrad became the first demonstrable case of the Soviets wresting air superiority from the Luftwaffe, and subsequently maintaining it. By the late fall of 1942, the Red Air Force had internalized the hard-fought lessons from the previous year and a half. They had reorganized their formations, developed new aircraft like the Lavochkin and Yakovlev fighters, and now had an experienced cadre of battle-hardened pilots. Moreover, by this point, the Soviets had discovered that "fighter-to-fighter combat was not very

Bf 109 pilots take a moment's rest during a lull in the fighting near Stalingrad.

In a vain attempt to keep the German 6th Army at Stalingrad resupplied, Ju 52 units (such as the one pictured here) worked beyond exhaustion and pushed their aircraft to the limits of their mechanical capacity. In the process, the Luftwaffe lost 266 Junkers transports and more than 200 other support aircraft in the failed attempt to rescue the 6th Army.

Collateral damage from the air war along the Eastern Front. Russian civilians scramble to extinguish the flames consuming their homes. Air raids from the Luftwaffe frequently set these homesteads ablaze.

Wings from a downed Soviet aircraft become an impromptu windbreak as local civilians try to cope with the war going on around them.

A burning engine from a Heinkel He 111, brought down by a Soviet fighter pilot near Stalingrad, 1943.

Soviet Lend-Lease planes at an Allied airfield in Iran, 1943. As the Soviets began to wrest their homeland back from the Wehrmacht, they received more Lend-Lease equipment from the Western Allies.

A P-40 Warhawk in Soviet service. The P-40 was a relative latecomer to the Red Air Force's Lend-Lease stable. Soviet pilots did not much care for what they considered to be an underpowered and underperforming "hand-me-down."

A MiG-3 interceptor with its winter camouflage paint scheme eroding from the elements. Although not a particularly well-received fighter, the Mikoyan-Gurevich plane performed well at higher altitudes.

Ilyushin Il-2s in flight. On July 5, 1943, some 132 Shturmoviks (part of a 500-plane task force) initiated a surprise attack on the Luftwaffe salient near Kharkov. Unfortunately for the Red Air Force, the attack on Kharkov failed.

A downed Soviet bomber near Kharkov, 1943.

German troops pose atop a single-seat variant of the Il-2. The warped propeller blades indicate that the plane's engine was still running when it crash-landed.

productive." According to historian Anthony Tucker-Jones, the Red Air Force consequently shifted its tactics to hunting enemy bombers and reconnaissance aircraft. This led to the aerial tactic of *zasada* (literally: "ambush").

In an unusual sight, the tail section of this Soviet bomber is all that remains after it met its fiery fate in the skies over Western Russia.

Still, Axis forces were mounting a heavy resistance in the air and on the ground. By mid-October 1942, the Luftwaffe received a fresh contingent of reinforcements from the Caucasus theater, and intensified its bombing campaign against the Soviet ground forces holding the west bank of the Volga River running through Stalingrad.

By the end of the month, Stukageschwader 1, 2, and 77 had destroyed the Soviet artillery batteries on the east bank of the Volga before turning their attention to the riverborne supply ferries that were trying to reinforce the defending ground units. With the Red Army contingent now forced into a 1,000-yard strip of land on the western bank of the Volga, the Ju 87s launched more than 1,200 dive-bombing missions to destroy the Soviet defenders.

The tide of the battle, however, was quickly turning in the Soviets' favor. As the Red Army began its counteroffensive across the Volga, three powerful air armies supported the

Another wrecked Ilyushin Il-2, 1943.

drive. On November 19, 1942, the revitalized Soviet artillery was so fierce that it prompted the Romanian 3rd Army (a German ally) to retreat in panic. Coming under the same fire, the German 6th Army now had a critical choice: make a "fighting retreat" or risk encirclement between the Don and Volga Rivers. Appealing to the Luftwaffe, Major General Arthur Schmidt, requested resupplying his entire field army by air.

His request was met with incredulity.

A German soldier inspects the remains of a Soviet aircraft downed in the woods.

A downed Il-2 lies canted to one side at the edge of a Russian cornfield. During the opening stages of the battle of Kursk, the Il-2 performed poorly due to its lack of fighter escort. Once accompanied into battle by the Yakovlev and Lavochkin fighters, however, the Shturmovik's survivability greatly improved.

Although Shturmovik losses were heavy along the Kursk battlefront, as this downed example illustrates, the Il-2 nonetheless became a more formidable adversary against German ground units as the Luftwaffe disappeared from the skies.

A Ju 87G prepares for combat, June 21, 1943.

Indeed, the Luftwaffe told Schmidt that resupplying a field army of 250,000 men by air was "stark staring madness." With resupply assets committed elsewhere on the North African front, and the deplorable weather in Russia, an aerial relief was all but impossible.

A few days later, Soviet ground forces captured the Luftwaffe's makeshift airfield at Kalach, near Stalingrad proper. Thereafter, fighters of the 16th Air Army went hunting the Luftwaffe's bomber and transport aircraft along the air corridors into Stalingrad. Over the next several days, dozens of German aircraft, including Ju 52s and Heinkel He 111s were destroyed by Soviet fighters. One such

Two Focke-Wulf pilots wish each other well before embarking on another mission, June 1944.

Two technicians perform routine maintenance on an Fw 190 between missions along the Eastern Front, June 1944.

A Yak pilot identified as L. Tomalchen poses for the camera after returning from a combat sortie in which he downed an He 111 and damaged a Ju 87 Stuka. Pilots of the Red Air Force were often hastily trained, but nevertheless thought of themselves as heroic defenders of Mother Russia.

Posing with a cigarette for added effect, Aleksander Pokryshkin was among the most distinguished fighter aces in Soviet history. With 59 confirmed kills, he achieved his "ace" status while flying the MiG-3. He later flew Yak-1s and P-39 Airacobras. On three separate occasions he was named "Hero of the Soviet Union."

engagement, on November 30, saw fighters from the 283rd Aviation Division down five Ju 52s along with a Bf 109.

Although the Red Air Force preferred hunting bombers to engaging in dogfights, Soviet fighters nevertheless fought valiantly in the skies over Stalingrad. The 296th Fighter Regiment, for example, achieved numerous victories with their Yakovlev Yak-1 fighters. Still, the fall and winter of 1942 proved to be a trying time for the Soviet fighters. As the commander of the 520th Fighter Regiment recalled, his 20 Yak-1s had a considerable baptism by fire against the Luftwaffe over Stalingrad. He wrote:

> Enemy bombers fly in groups of 10–30 aircraft, and in rare cases they are covered by two or three Me 109s. They approach their target in close vee formation at 1,500–2,000 meters [4,900–6,500 feet] altitude and then break formation, form a circle and release their bombs from a slanting dive. When our fighters arrive, they return to the close vee formation and then flee to their territory. The Messerschmitts patrol in pairs, spaced at an altitude of 1,500–3,500 meters [4,900–11,000 feet], often attacking abruptly. They open fire from the rear hemisphere, firing accurately from 50–100 meters [160–325 feet]. Multiple observations show that the enemy fighters persistently chase ours to their very airfields, sometimes attacking even though they are short of fuel.

Understandably, the dogfights over Stalingrad were intense. And although the Red Air Force was tallying their victories, they nevertheless suffered great losses, especially during the opening months of August and September. The biggest contributor to these early losses was the Yak-1 itself, flying against the F-4 and G-2 variants of the Bf 109. For its part, the

Soviet ground crew prepare an Il-2M for take-off. The "M" variant of the Il-2 featured a rear-facing 12.7mm machine gun in addition to the forward-facing anti-tank armaments.

German troops inspect two examples of an early-model, single-seat Shturmovik; one crash-landed, the other abandoned.

Yak-1 often caught fire when hit by incendiary rounds to the fuel tanks or cockpit. Although the composite-wooden structure facilitated its ease of maintenance, it left the plane horribly underprotected. And due to the cockpit's poor visibility, pilots preferred to leave their canopy open during flight. This of course left the pilots more vulnerable to enemy gunfire.

Heavy losses were also attributed to the inadequate training that many Soviet pilots received. To replenish the ever-dwindling manpower on the Eastern Front, "flying schools were told to cut the minimum number of hours required to train replacement pilots." Most of these poorly trained Soviet pilots were killed on their first combat missions. At Stalingrad, throughout late 1942, young aviators flying upgraded Yak-7s were usually shot down between their fifth and eighth combat sorties. Given the accelerated pace of their training, and the high turnover in combat personnel, many of the Soviet pilots arriving at the front felt "very unsure of their own abilities, and as they tried their best not to lose their flight leaders, they could not monitor the situation in the air." Thus, many of these novice pilots didn't notice enemy bandits on their tail until they had already been fired upon.

Despite these losses, the Soviet counteroffensive of 1942–43 highlighted the heroism and tenacity of several distinguished pilots, many of whom were women. Although there were no formal restrictions against women in combat roles, the Soviet government tried to discourage women from fighting on the frontlines. Still, Soviet women signed up in droves to support the war effort. In several instances, they served in all-female units. One such example was the 586th Fighter Aviation Regiment. Staffed by female aviators flying Yak-1s, the 586th Regiment initially defended the skies over Saratov, wherein Lieutenant Valeria Khomyakova achieved the regiment's first combat victory, downing a Ju 88A from the Luftwaffe's III./ KG 76 on the night on September 24, 1942.

The women of the 586th arrived on the Stalingrad front shortly thereafter. Two of the regiment's pilots, Yekaterina Budanova and Lydia Litvyak, shot down a dozen German planes by August 1943. Litvyak was the highest-scoring Soviet female ace of the war and, to this day, she is the most successful female fighter pilot in history. Officially credited with 12 kills, some historians estimate that her actual kill record was closer to 16, nine of which were Bf 109s. She was killed in August 1943 when her plane was shot down during the battle of Kursk. She was only 21 at the time of her death. Her comrade and fellow female ace, Yekaterina Budanova, was likewise shot down in 1943. Both women were posthumously awarded the highest honors for Soviet military service.

Alexander Efimov, pictured here in 1944, was a prominent Il-2 Shturmovik pilot, flying 288 sorties. His impressive kill record included 85 German aircraft destroyed while they were still on the ground. Efimov also confirmed eight enemy planes killed in air-to-air combat, a rare feat for an Il-2.

In Profile:
Lydia Litvyak
August 18, 1921–August 1, 1943

Unlike the Western Allies, the Soviet Union had no formal restrictions against women in combat. Still, women were assigned to all-female units. Among the most prominent of the Soviet Union's female flyers was Lydia Litvyak, nicknamed the "White Rose of Stalingrad." Born in Moscow in 1921, Lydia developed an interest in aviation at an early age. She joined a local flying club at the age of 14, and by the end of her teenage years, she was a licensed flight instructor. By the time World War II erupted on the Eastern Front, she had trained nearly 50 pilots. After joining the Soviet Air Force, Litvyak distinguished herself in aerial combat, scoring 12 air-to-air victories by the age of 21. She was killed on August 1, 1943 when her Yak-1 fighter was shot down near Dmitryevka.

A German soldier inspects the wreckage of a Soviet SB-2 light bomber. The fuselage of the bomber is riddled with anti-aircraft shell holes. As the Luftwaffe fighter force dwindled in numbers, the Wehrmacht began to rely more heavily on ground-based air defense batteries to fend off the Red Air Force.

Another downed Soviet bomber near the Russian border. With the German Army showing its heels, and the Soviet military in hot pursuit, the Germans became increasingly more desperate in their attempts to keep the Red Army at bay.

Soviet wreckage attracts more German sightseers.

As for the 586th Regiment itself, the unit converted from Yak-1s to Yak-9s in 1943. By the end of the war, the regiment's combat record stood at 4,419 sorties and 38 enemy aircraft destroyed.

Other fighter aces who emerged during this time included Aleksandr Pokryshkin and Nelson Stepanyan. Pokryshkin's wartime record includes 156 aerial engagements and 59 kills. Initially flying MiG-3s, he later converted to Yak-1s, and later flew Lend-Lease P-39 Airacobras. He had been in the sky since the first day of *Barbarossa* and, by the end of the war, he was commanding the 9th Guards Fighter Aviation Division. He ultimately survived the Great Patriotic War and was awarded Hero of the Soviet Union three times.

Stepanyan was an Il-2 Shturmovik pilot who, before his death in 1944, flew 239 combat missions, destroying 680 enemy vehicles, 53 naval vessels, and 27 enemy aircraft in various missions across the Eastern Front. Armenian by birth, Stepanyan was assigned to the 57th Air Division where he initially saw combat in the skies over Leningrad. During the critical year of the Soviet counteroffensive, 1942/3, Stepanyan's ground-attack record became the stuff of legend—it was reported that he had single-handedly destroyed 78 enemy trucks, 63 anti-aircraft guns, 36 rail cars, 67 tanks, five ammunition dumps, and five bridges. In 1943, he was promoted to major and assumed command of the 47th Fighter Division, renowned for its heroic offensives in Theodosia and the Crimea. He was shot down once behind enemy lines but, upon a fortuitous meeting with Soviet partisans, he was able to find his way back to friendly territory, where he immediately resumed his flight duties. Stepanyan continued racking up victories until December 1944 when, on a patrol in Latvia, his Il-2 was hit by enemy ground fire. Determined to take a few of the enemy down with him, Stepanyan died when he crashed his ailing plane into an enemy ship.

Meanwhile, the Luftwaffe's attempt to maintain the air corridor into Stalingrad came at a terrible price. Throughout that winter, the Red Air Force claimed 162 fighters, 227

A crash-landed Yakovlev Yak-9 in Finland, September 1944.

An American pilot stands alongside two Soviet aviators in front of a Lend-Lease P-39 Airacobra. Throughout the war, a handful of Americans served as advisors to Soviet units operating Lend-Lease equipment. The alliance, however, was short-lived. After their common enemy in Hitler had been defeated, US–Soviet relations devolved into the "Cold War," an ideological struggle that would span nearly two generations.

An American B-17 Flying Fortress from the 99th Bombardment Group sits alongside a group of Yakovlev Yak-9 fighters at a joint Allied airfield, while their aircrews swap stories, 1944.

bombers, and 676 transport aircraft. From November 1942 to January 1943, the Germans admitted losing 490 aircraft—roughly the equivalent of an entire air corps. These were losses from which the Luftwaffe would never recover. On the ground, meanwhile, the Red Army had smashed through the Romanian, Hungarian, and Italian contingents that had been supporting the German advance. By February, the remaining Axis units had exhausted their food and ammunition. The tattered remnants of the German 6th Army surrendered on February 2. For the Luftwaffe, however, their aerial transport capabilities had been damaged beyond repair.

As 1942 dragged on, two opposing fighter planes took center stage over the Eastern Front: the Lavochkin La-5 and the Focke-Wulf Fw 190. These opposing numbers met for the first time during the fall of 1942. By this time, the Focke-Wulf had been in frontline service for more than a year. As a fighter and latter-day ground-attack aircraft, the Fw 190 was a force to be reckoned with. As the underpowered Stuka began withdrawing from frontline service, the Fw 190 took its place. The La-5, however, endured a number of "growing pains" as it debuted on the frontlines of the Eastern theater. Indeed, the first batch of production La-5s had been rushed into the fighting over Stalingrad.

Assigned to the 287th Fighter Aviation Division, the La-5 showed potential, but was beset by multiple design and performance problems. Pilots often said the La-5 was more difficult to fly than the Yak-1 or LaGG-3, citing its heavy weight among other factors. Soviet pilots were, however, impressed by the durability of its engine, "and the protection it offered during frontal attacks." In terms of speed and maneuverability, Soviet flyers commented that

In another jubilant US–Soviet photograph, an American airman poses with the crew of a Petlyakov Pe-2 bomber. Much like the Luftwaffe's Ju 87, the Pe-2 carried dive brakes that could control the aircraft's speed during the complex choreography of dive-bombing.

the La-5 lagged behind the Bf 109, stating in 1942 that "We have to engage only in defensive combat actions. The enemy is superior in altitude and, therefore, had a more favorable position from which to attack."

During their initial encounters with the Fw 190 A-3 and A-4 variants, however, the La-5 fared much better. The Focke-Wulf still had the edge, but just barely. According to historian Dmitriy Khazanov:

As part of Operation *Bagration*, the assault into Byelorussia, a Pe-2 crew conducts a final pre-mission briefing. During the campaign, Pe-2 bombers from the 1st Air Army flew some 160 sorties in support of Soviet ground forces.

> Soviet pilots reported that the Lavochkin could stay with—but not overtake—an Fw 190 in horizontal flight at low altitude, and their performance was similar when maneuvering in the same plane. When chasing or evading an Fw 190 in a climb, the La-5 (which was half a ton lighter) enjoyed some advantage. However, its maneuverability at speeds in excess of 250mph left a lot to be desired in comparison with the Fw 190. Most pilots felt that the ailerons and elevators were

By 1945, the vaunted Fw 190 was in its twilight. The La-7 had been gaining an edge on the Focke-Wulf since the former's introduction in 1944. The tired faces of the Luftwaffe pilots provide mute testimony that Hitler's battle-hardened airmen were now becoming battle-weary.

The Fw 190 still retained a slight edge over the La-5.

> particularly heavy when turning tightly at higher speeds and when exiting a dive. This in turn meant that only physically strong pilots could hope to get the best out of the early La-5s when engaging enemy fighters.

What truly gave the Fw 190 its edge over the La-5, however, was the comparative combat experience of the Luftwaffe pilots. Indeed, the pilots who took the Focke-Wulf into combat along the Eastern Front were grizzled veterans of the blitzkrieg campaign and the aerial skirmishes over the English Channel. Most of them had been fighting the Red Air Force for more than a year, and had achieved "ace" status of five or more kills. Moreover, it seemed that the Luftwaffe pilots would change their tactics from sortie to sortie. As Soviet ace Major Andrei Baklan recalled: "During my four years of fighting the Luftwaffe, I failed to discern any particular pattern to the tactical formations and tactics employed by enemy aces. There was no set form of combat that they followed, hence the fact that they were so dangerous."

Bf 109s prepare for what might be one of their final sorties in defense of the Fatherland. By 1945, many fighter units had been grounded due to lack of fuel and spare parts.

Still, the La-5 mounted a heavy resistance against the Fw 190 aces. For example, on August 28, 1943, Captain Ivan Kozich and his wingman, Junior Lieutenant Storozhko, of 721st Fighter Aviation Regiment were on a reconnaissance mission west of Orel in their La-5Fs when they were suddenly ambushed by eight Fw 190s. Kozich and Storozhko noticed that the eight Focke-Wulfs had split themselves into two groups of four—the first group approaching them from behind at 12,000 feet, while the second group vectored from the right, approximately 2,000 feet higher.

Kozich turned his La-5 towards the trailing group of Fw 190s, firing a burst from his autocannon into the lead aircraft. His initial salvo missed but, undeterred, Kozich turned his attention to the leader's left wingman, scoring a direct hit. By the time the second group of Fw 190s had closed in, Kozich pulled back the throttle, taking the La-5 into a tight diving turn and placing him directly behind all four of the enemy's aircraft. From a distance of 150 feet, Kozich fired on his second Focke-Wulf of the day, skillfully downing the bandit on the opposite side of the flight leader. Kozich's wingman, Storozhko, however, was shot down by one of the lingering Focke-Wulfs after a brief but intense dogfight. Kozich, who had already been named a "Hero of the Soviet Union," survived this engagement and the war. By VE Day, he had been credited with 16 individual kills.

Curiously, in the summer of 1943, a wayward La-5 made a forced landing on a German airfield, giving the Luftwaffe its much-desired opportunity to fly and deconstruct the Soviet fighter. Hans-Werner Lerche, the test pilot who flew the captured La-5, wrote a detailed evaluation. He noted that the La-5FN variant excelled at altitudes below 9,000 feet, but was hamstrung by a short range and low endurance. Lerche also found the engine controls problematic—mainly because each function (i.e. mixture, throttle, radiator and cowl flaps, etc.) was controlled by separate levers that the pilot had to adjust during flight. Trying to control each of these in combat would, understandably, detract from the pilot's situational awareness. By comparison, the German BMW 801 aircraft engine could automatically control all of these settings from a single lever. And although the La-5 was stable in flight, the German evaluators found that the rudder was insufficient for the airframe and that the plane's horizontal turning time was too slow by Western standards—25 seconds.

As a result of Lerche's evaluation, Fw 190 pilots were encouraged to draw the Lavochkin to higher altitudes, then conduct a sharp dive followed by a high-speed shallow climb. This would allow the Focke-Wulf to avoid prolonged turning engagements. The Soviets, meanwhile, aware of the same shortcomings noted by Lerche, had already begun development of an improved Lavochkin: the La-7.

In the forward fuselage of an He 111, a navigator plots his course on another bombing run.

In Profile:
586th Fighter Aviation Regiment

Side view of the Yakovlev Yak-1.

A Yakovlev Yak-7A fighter stands ready for another sortie. Although the Yak-series fighters got off to a shaky start during World War II, they were among the most well-respected Soviet aircraft by the end of the war.

During the Great Patriotic War, Soviet women served mostly in all-female units. The 586th was one of the three Soviet all-female aviation regiments founded by Marina Raskova. The 586th was initially equipped with Yakovlev Yak-1s, but later converted to Yak-7s and Yak-9s. Most of their sorties included defensive counter-air missions, conducting aerial patrols over various installations. But whether flying offensive or defensive air patrols, the 586th Fighter Aviation Regiment continually distinguished itself in combat. In fact, the regiment yielded two of the Soviet Union's most distinguished female pilots: Lydia Litvyak and Yekaterina Budanova, both of whom were posthumously awarded the highest honors for valor in the skies over Russia.

Turning the Tide

1943 proved to be the critical year of the air campaign over Western Russia—due in no small part to the Soviet victory at the battle of Kursk. The six-week engagement at Kursk still resonates as the largest tank battle in history. In the air, however, the conflict was just as brutal. Hitler's plan was to smash the Red Army at Kursk, and regain the initiative along the Eastern Front. Although the Western Allies had yet to invade the European mainland, they had already gained a foothold in North Africa and were preparing to invade Sicily.

All told, Hitler had two options: (1) pacify the Soviet front, or (2) fight a protracted two-front war in his own backyard. Thus, to assist the Führer in accomplishing the former, the Luftwaffe diverted every spare asset it could muster.

Flying prominently over the battlefield at Kursk was the Il-2 Shturmovik—Stalin's vaunted "Flying Tank." Since the start of the air war, Il-2 pilots had developed a deadly technique for trapping enemy panzers—the "Circle of Death." Under this technique, Il-2 formations would maintain a circular flight pattern above the German panzer units. Each Shturmovik would then take turns peeling off from the circle, initiating its own strafing run. This kept the German ground units under constant fire and, during the battle of Kursk, it facilitated the demise of the 2nd and 3rd Panzer Divisions.

The Luftwaffe, for its part, mustered nearly 2,000 aircraft for the battle—including various fighters, fighter-bombers, and ground-attack aircraft. Meanwhile, the Red Air Force, energized by the victory at Stalingrad, decided to bring the fight to Hitler's airmen. Indeed, on July 5, 1943, just as the Luftwaffe contingent was about to depart from its forward airbases near Kharkov, some 285 Soviet fighters and 132 Shturmoviks descended upon them. Representing the 2nd and 17th Air Armies, these Soviet flyers were attempting to destroy the German bombers before they got within striking distance of Kursk. Unfortunately for the Soviets, German radar alerted the

The tail of a Soviet bomber lies derelict in a German field. By the end of 1944, it was apparent that the Wehrmacht could no longer keep the Red Army or the Red Air Force at bay. It then became a question of how long German forces could delay their inevitable defeat.

A German souvenir hunter cuts the Red Star roundel from the remains of a Soviet aircraft.

Luftwaffe of the incoming aerial assault. German fighters forward-stationed at Mikoyanovka and Kharkov were scrambled to intercept the Soviet aircraft. What ensued was the largest single aerial battle of the of the Eastern Front.

As General Hans Seidemann recalled: "It was a rare spectacle; everywhere planes were burning and crashing. In no time at all, some 120 Soviet aircraft were downed. Our own losses were so small as to represent total victory, for the consequence was complete German

An ailing Ju 88 advances towards the Byelorussian front. Although the Luftwaffe's efforts were inspiring, these German air squadrons were, by now, no match for the Red juggernaut.

air control in the 8th Air Corps sector." In other words, it was a catastrophic blow to the Red Air Force, one that cost them air superiority over the southern flank of Kursk. Indeed, their optimistic preemptive attack against the Luftwaffe's forward airbases had ended in disaster.

At first, it seemed that the Red Air Force wouldn't be able to repel the Luftwaffe from Kursk. Along the northern sector of the battlefront, two Soviet fighter corps had failed to stem the influx of German bandits—losing more than 100 aircraft to prowling Fw 190s. To make matters worse, the initial waves of Shturmoviks and Pe-2s were failing to break through to their targets. Because these initial sorties lacked fighter escorts, they were easy pickings for marauding Bf 109s and Focke-Wulfs.

To remedy the situation, however, the Red Air Force responded by sending regimental-sized elements aloft. Thus, due to sheer numbers, the Il-2s and Pe-2s were able to break through and began inflicting heavy losses on German ground units in and around Kursk. By July 8, 1943, the Soviets had slowed the German advance, and the Luftwaffe's upper hand was beginning to falter.

By July 19, 1943, with the German offensive having been stalled, Soviet tanks reached the city of Khotinez. This enabled Soviet ground forces to cut the railway between Bryansk and Orel—a critical lifeline in the Germans' forward logistics network. The Luftwaffe, however, was determined not to have a repeat of Stalingrad. Thus, the Ju 87s stationed at Karachev got airborne, spearheading an intense dive-bombing campaign against the incoming Soviet tanks. The brief aerial attack was somewhat of a miracle—for it was the first time that a Soviet tank force had been beaten back from the air. Although the Stukas and their stablemates had prevented an encirclement of their ground-based comrades, this show of force was the last hurrah for the Luftwaffe on the Eastern Front.

Luftwaffe technicians prepare an Fw 190 for combat.

Focke-Wulf Fw 190s in Finland, 1944. For most of World War II, Finland was one of Nazi Germany's most prominent allies, with the Finns harboring an understandable resentment of the Soviets following the Winter War of 1940. Finnish forces regularly fought alongside the Wehrmacht and, prior to the Finnish treaty with Moscow in late 1944, the Finns allowed Nazi forces to operate from bases in Finland.

The crew of a Sukhoi Su-2 receive their final instructions before another combat mission, 1944. Although Sukhoi would later become a powerhouse in Soviet and Russian aerospace, the design bureau was a minor contributor during the Great Patriotic War. Sukhoi's only tactical aircraft to see action on the Eastern Front was the Su-2, and only in limited numbers. Sukhoi developed the Su-6 as a ground-attack aircraft, but the Red Air Force ultimately selected the Il-2 Shturmovik for its attack squadrons.

Meanwhile, farther south, the Red Army stormed into Kharkov while the Red Air Force hammered the German panzer units trying to reinforce the area. On August 23, the Soviets recaptured Kharkov and the Red Air Force occupied its airfields. With the Luftwaffe now on the run, the ailing bomber and fighter units withdrew to their airbases in Kremenchug, Dnepropetrovsk, and Mirgorod. In doing so, the Luftwaffe commanders hoped they could regroup and reinforce the German defenses along the Dnieper River. By now, however, the remaining Luftwaffe assets had been spread too thin. Thus, they were no longer combat-effective.

The German Army was soundly defeated at the battle of Kursk. The 2nd and 4th Panzer Armies were effectively in shambles, and the Luftwaffe had limped out of the fight with several hundred aircraft destroyed. It was a defeat from which the combined forces of Hitler's war machine would never recover.

As the Red Air Force began driving the Luftwaffe back towards the German hinterland, Joseph Stalin continued supplementing his airmen with gifts from the Lend-Lease Program. As mentioned previously, the Soviets made extensive use of the Hawker Hurricane and P-39 Airacobra in their campaigns against the Wehrmacht. In 1944, however, the Red Air Force graciously accepted the P-63 Kingcobra and the vaunted P-47 Lightning. Rounding out these new deliveries were nearly 2,000 P-40 Warhawks—none of which were well received as the Soviets considered them "cast-offs" in favor of the P-51 Mustang. However, as Soviet fighters like the La-7 and Yak-7/9 gained parity with the Luftwaffe, more emphasis was placed on acquiring Lend-Lease bombers. To that end, the Americans provided nearly 3,000 A-20 light bombers and 862 B-25 medium bombers.

Fall of the Fatherland

By the fall of 1943, the Eastern Front was no longer a priority for the Luftwaffe, or the Wehrmacht at large. By necessity, it couldn't be a priority. For by now, Hitler had to ward off the RAF and the US Army Air Forces. By the spring of 1944, the number of serviceable German aircraft in Russia had fallen to 1,800. Despite increased aircraft production, there was a high turnover rate of pilots on both fronts of the war. The growing Allied air superiority over both fronts meant that the Luftwaffe's days were numbered. Indeed, the best that Hitler's airmen could hope for was temporary air superiority on a localized basis.

June 1944. Destroyed vehicles of the German 9th Army, following Operation *Bagration*, the Soviets' drive into Byelorussia. The devastation seen in this photograph is the handiwork of the Soviet 16th Air Army.

Soviet soldiers posing proudly by a destroyed German plane. By 1945, the tables had turned sharply against the Axis, as the Soviets penetrated the heart of the Reich.

Conversely, the Red Air Force seemed to be growing month by month. Throughout the last half of 1943, the number of Soviet aircraft had plateaued at around 8,300 airframes. By the middle of 1944, however, that number had risen to 13,500 and, by April 1945, the Red Air Force boasted some 17,000 operational aircraft.

By the summer of 1944, the Luftwaffe's eastern salient consisted of only three air fleets which amongst them had fewer than 1,700 operational aircraft. The Ju 88s and He 111s assigned to this air contingent continued bombing Soviet rail lines and supply depots. Although, by this point, the Germans had effectively lost air superiority over Russia, the Luftwaffe still tried to interdict their troop movements. These bombers continued targeting Soviet infrastructure points until fuel shortages forced their deactivation in late 1944.

Meanwhile, the summer of 1944 saw the Red Air Force initiate Operation *Bagration*—the strategic push to into Byelorussia (modern-day Belarus), and "the largest tactical concentration of Soviet air power to date." For the invasion of Byelorussia, the Red Air Force amassed more than 5,300 combat aircraft and an additional 1,007 bombers. Taken together, this aerial task force comprised 21 fighter divisions, 14 ground-attack divisions, and eight bomber divisions. This accounted for more than 2,300 Soviet fighters (including the new Lavochkin La-7), and 1,744 Il-2 Shturmoviks.

On the night of June 22, 1944—the third anniversary of Operation *Barbarossa*—the Red Air Force conducted nearly 1,000 bombing runs on German positions along the

Byelorussian front, striking critical airfields and the surrounding rail lines. The following morning, Pe-2 bombers from the 1st Air Army capitalized on the previous night's success, conducting some 160 bombing runs during the early daylight hours. Meanwhile, Soviet ground artillery and Katyusha rocket batteries pummeled the frontline Wehrmacht positions before the Il-2 Shturmovik regiments flew in on their signature strafing runs. This precipitated Soviet ground forces moving in to seize the key terrain needed to overrun Army Group Center.

After the success of Operation *Bagration*, the Red Army turns its attention to Warsaw, then Berlin. Ten Soviet air armies supported that final push into the Fatherland. With a total of 15,815 aircraft (including the latest Yak-9s and La-7s), the Soviets pounded the Germans' frontier defenses. The Soviet bombers and Shturmoviks of the 16th Air Army led the way in clearing the path to Berlin, especially in their attacks on the Seelow Heights. During that drive to the German capital, the Red Air Force flew some 92,000 sorties, many of which were at night.

The Allied bombing of Berlin, 1945.

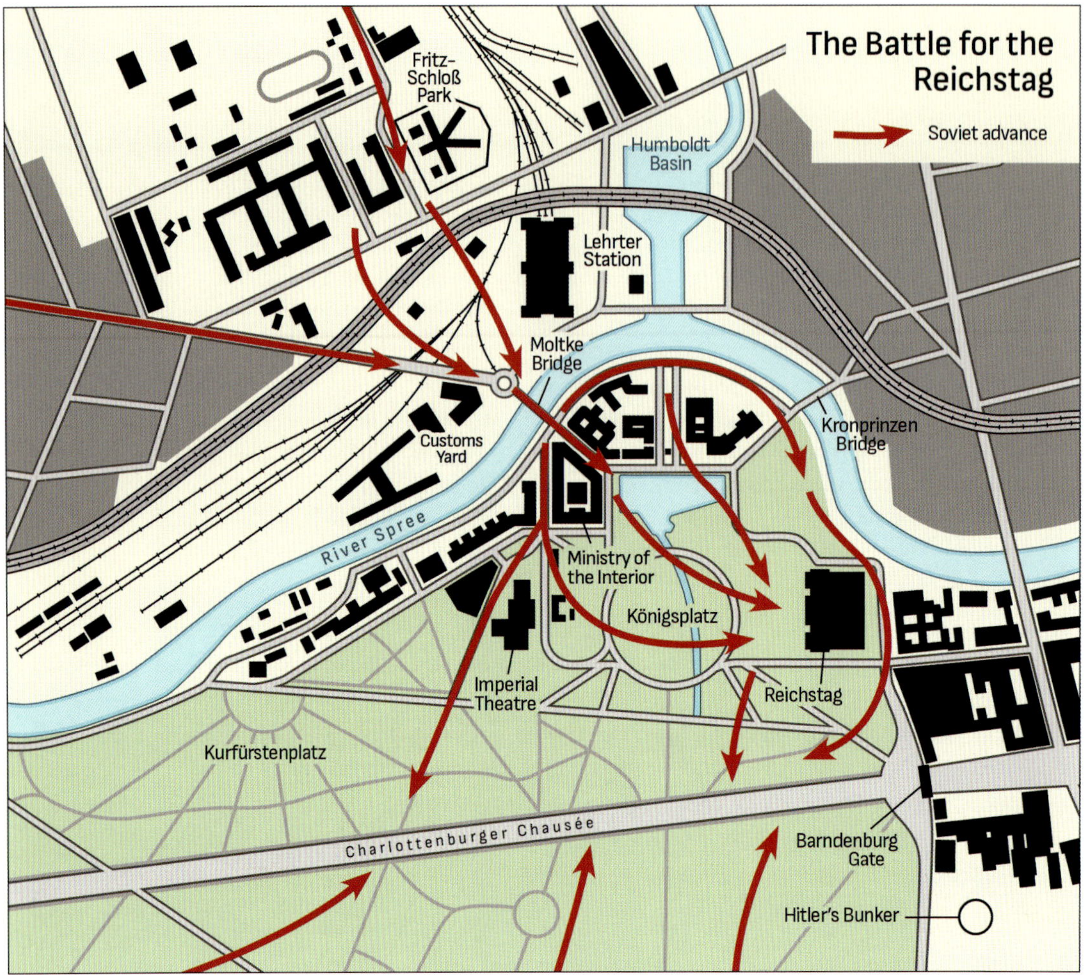

Following Operation *Bagration* in 1944, the Soviets gained a foothold within the borders of the Reich. By the late spring of 1945, the Red Army and Red Air Force had descended upon the German capital. This map shows the air and ground avenues of attack as Soviet forces poured into the center of Berlin. From the air, Soviet planes such as the Ilyushin Il-2 pounded the German defenses from March 1945 until the city was subdued that May.

Meanwhile, the new-and-improved Lavochkin La-7 made its combat debut in August 1944. At roughly the same time, the Red Air Force began mimicking the "free hunt" tactics used by the Luftwaffe. Under the "free hunt" methodology, pilots would avoid protracted dogfights, opting instead to conduct rapid strikes on an enemy formation, then escape under cover from the clouds or the sun.

Among the new La-7 jockeys was Captain Nikolay Skomorokhov, whose combat record included 46 confirmed kills, including 18 Focke-Wulfs. By 1944, he had been twice decorated as a "Hero of the Soviet Union." Having flown the earlier LaGG-3 and La-5, he had been on the frontlines since the fall of 1942. While flying with the 164th Fighter Aviation Regiment, he took his first La-7 into combat in March 1945. He recalled his first engagements in the La-7 as such:

> Having initially sat in the cockpit and familiarized myself with the aircraft's idiosyncrasies, I then took off. I performed a few rolls and vertical climbs—this aircraft was a beast! My conversion ended there. A short while later our ground-based fighter controller directed us to the Kapolnash–Nieka region, where we spotted ten Fw 190s in front of us that were about to attack our troops. There was no time to waste. I immediately dispatched an aircraft that was flying on its own and then opened fire on a second machine. This caused panic to set in amongst the surviving Focke-Wulf pilots, who scattered in different directions and raced back home at low altitude. Eight more Fw 190s then appeared … and I again managed to shoot down a fighter. Having seen the loss of their comrades, the remaining fascist pilots abandoned their attacks and fled.

With the advent of the La-7, the Soviets now had a fighter that could unquestionably stand toe to toe against any plane in the Luftwaffe.

A Soviet soldier raises the flag of the USSR over the Reichstag in Berlin, May 2, 1945. With the German capital now in Soviet hands, the war was effectively over for Nazi Germany.

Aftermath

During the final battle over Berlin, the Luftwaffe held out until the very end. Although flying at barely a fraction of their former size, Hitler's aircrews took to the sky in more than 1,300 engagements, losing 527 aircraft in the defense of their capital city. Meanwhile, Hitler himself grew ever more frantic. With the Americans closing in from the west, and the Soviets closing in from the east, he committed suicide on April 30, 1945. Seven days later, the Wehrmacht surrendered.

In 1939, the Luftwaffe had been the premier air force in Europe. By May 1945, however, it was but a hollow shell of its former self—with barely enough fuel to keep its surviving planes in the air. All told, the Germans lost nearly 40,000 aircraft in combat. The cost in manpower, however, was much higher. According to the General Staff of the Wehrmacht, the Luftwaffe's casualty record amounted to 138,596 killed and 156,132 missing by 1945. After the war, the Luftwaffe was disbanded by the Allied Commission in 1946, and outlawed along with all things Nazi. Many prominent members of the Luftwaffe were tried for war crimes, including Hermann Göring himself. Some who escaped the gallows at Nuremberg later found their way into the West German Air Force or the Luftstreitkräfte of East Germany. The air force of the now reunified Germany is once again called the "Luftwaffe" but it bears no operational continuity or heraldry from the World War II-era force.

In the final analysis, the Red Air Force dominated the Luftwaffe not through superior tactics or equipment, but through sheer numbers, force, and dogged determination. That the Soviet military recovered as quickly as after *Barbarossa* is nothing short of a miracle.

A scrapyard for the Luftwaffe. Following Germany's surrender on May 8, 1945, most of the Luftwaffe's surviving equipment was destroyed as part of the "de-Nazification" process.

Although straddled by the brutal and heavy-handed rule of Joseph Stalin, these Soviet flyers took to the sky, defending their homeland with a zeal that shocked even the most hardened Luftwaffe pilots. Entering the fight with inferior equipment and subpar tactics, the Red Air Force quickly adapted to the situation, while throwing every piece of available manpower and materiel at the invading Axis forces.

Some historians have concluded that while the Red Army facilitated Germany's destruction on the ground, that the Red Air Force was comparatively less effective. These same historians claim that it was the RAF and the US Army Air Forces that truly killed the Luftwaffe. While the Western Allies' air forces are not to be slighted, the reality is that the Red Air Force, according to historian Anthony Tucker-Jones "evolved and grew into a war-winning instrument of destruction." It has been said that the lessons best learned are those learned under fire. This certainly holds true for the Red Air Force. Stalin's airmen had to learn to protect and improve their aircraft while on the brink of total collapse. In 1941, the Red Air Force was losing one aircraft for every 32 sorties. By 1945, that ratio had fallen to one aircraft for every 165.

Throughout the war, the Red Air Force and PVO flew more than 3 million sorties, dropping more than 600,000 tons of ordnance. Taking a critical look at their role in the conflict, the Red Air Force was set to develop two new capabilities: long-range strategic bombing and jet aircraft. Both developments became cornerstones of Soviet aviation during the Cold War, with design bureaus like Tupelov and Mikoyan-Gurevich taking the lead. But like its erstwhile adversary in Nazi Germany, the Red Air Force would eventually be disbanded as well. Following the breakup of the Soviet Union in 1991, the assets belonging to the Soviet Air Forces were parceled out to the various successor states. Today's Russian Air Force, however, continues the legacy of the latter-day Soviet airmen.

Decommissioned Focke-Wulf Fw 190s await demolition at a temporary scrapyard in Germany. Today, only a handful of vintage aircraft from the Luftwaffe era have survived, most of which are no longer airworthy.

Further Reading

Bergström, Christer. *Bagration to Berlin: The Final Air Battles in the East, 1944–1945*. Shepperton: Ian Allen Publishing, 2008.

Bergström, Christer, and Andrey Mikhailov. *Black Cross/Red Star—Air War Over the Eastern Front: Volume 1, Operation Barbarossa, 1941*, 2nd ed. Pacifica, CA: Pacifica Press, 2000.

Bergström, Christer, and Andrey Mikhailov. *Black Cross/Red Star—Air War Over the Eastern Front, Volume 2: Resurgence, January–June 1942*, 2nd ed. Pacifica, CA: Pacifica Press, 2001.

Bergström, Christer. *Black Cross/Red Star—Air War Over the Eastern Front: Volume 3, Everything for Stalingrad*. Hamilton, MT: Eagle Editions, 2006.

Bergström, Christer. *Black Cross/Red Star—Air War Over the Eastern Front: Volume 4: Stalingrad to Kuban 1942–1943*. Eskilstuna: Vaktel Forlag, 2019.

Hardesty, Von, and Ilya Grinberg. *Red Phoenix Rising: The Soviet Air Force in World War II*. Lawrence, KS: University Press of Kansas, 2012.

Hooton, E. R. *War over the Steppes: The Air Campaigns on the Eastern Front 1941–45*. Oxford: Osprey Publishing, 2016.

Khazanov, Dmitriy. *MiG-3 Aces of World War 2*. Oxford: Osprey Publishing, 2013.

Khazanov, Dmitriy, and Aleksander Medved. *Bf 109E/F vs Yak-1/7: Eastern Front 1941–42*. Oxford: Osprey Publishing, 2015.

Khazanov, Dmitriy, and Aleksander Medved. *La-5/7 vs Fw 190: Eastern Front 1942–45*. Oxford: Osprey Publishing, 2011.

Loza, Dmitriĭ F. *Attack of the Airacobras: Soviet Aces, American P-39's and the Air War Against Germany*. Lawrence, KS: University Press of Kansas, 2002.

Mellinger, George. *LaGG & Lavochkin Aces of World War 2*. Oxford: Osprey Publishing, 2012.

Mellinger, George. *Yakovlev Aces of World War 2*. Oxford: Osprey Publishing, 2012.

Moore, Jason N. *Il-2 Shturmovik: Red Avenger*. Brimscombe: Fonthill Media, 2017.

Page, Neil. *Day Fighter Aces of the Luftwaffe 1939-42*. Oxford: Casemate Publishers, 2020.

Page, Neil. Day *Fighter Aces of the Luftwaffe 1942-45*. Oxford: Casemate Publishers, 2020.

Plokhy, Serhii. *Forgotten Bastards of the Eastern Front: American Airmen Behind the Soviet Lines and the Collapse of the Grand Alliance*. New York: Oxford University Press (USA), 2019.

Tucker-Jones, Anthony. *The Eastern Front Air War, 1941–1945*. Barnsley: Pen and Sword, 2016.

Weal, John. *Junkers Ju 87 Stukageschwader of the Russian Front*. Oxford: Osprey Publishing, 2012.

Weal, John. *Focke-Wulf Fw 190 Aces of the Russian Front*. Oxford: Osprey Publishing, 1995.

Index